NEW DIRECTIONS FOR HIGHER EDUCATION

Martin Kramer
EDITOR-IN-CHIEF

Internationalizing Higher Education: Building Vital Programs on Campuses

Bruce W. Speck
Austin Peay State University

Beth H. Carmical
The University of North Carolina at Pembroke

EDITORS

Number 117, Spring 2002

JOSSEY-BASS
San Francisco

INTERNATIONALIZING HIGHER EDUCATION: BUILDING VITAL PROGRAMS ON CAMPUSES
Bruce W. Speck, Beth H. Carmical (eds.)
New Directions for Higher Education, no. 117
Martin Kramer, Editor-in-Chief

Microfilm copies of issues and articles are available in 16mm and 35mm, as well as microfiche in 105mm, through University Microfilms Inc., 300 North Zeeb Road, Ann Arbor, Michigan 48106-1346.

ISSN 0271-0560   electronic ISSN 1536-0741   ISBN 0-7879-6290-2

NEW DIRECTIONS FOR HIGHER EDUCATION is part of The Jossey-Bass Higher and Adult Education Series and is published quarterly by Wiley Subscription Services, Inc., a Wiley company, at Jossey-Bass, 989 Market Street, San Francisco, California 94103-1741. Periodicals postage paid at San Francisco, California, and at additional mailing offices. Postmaster: Send address changes to New Directions for Higher Education, Jossey-Bass, 989 Market Street, San Francisco, California 94103-1741

SUBSCRIPTIONS cost $60 for individuals and $131 for institutions, agencies, and libraries. See ordering information page at end of book.

EDITORIAL CORRESPONDENCE should be sent to the Editor-in-Chief, Martin Kramer, 2807 Shasta Road, Berkeley, California 94708-2011.

Cover photograph and random dot by Richard Blair/Color & Light © 1990.

Jossey-Bass Web address: www.josseybass.com

Printed in the United States of America on acid-free recycled paper containing at least 20 percent postconsumer waste.

CONTENTS

Editors' Notes

September 11, 2001 marked the beginning of a new era in international relationships. The attack on the World Trade Center in New York City prompted the U.S. government to draw a line in the sand, inviting every government in the world who opposes terrorism to join America on the right side of the line. However, drawing such a line, although symbolic of a black-and-white approach to terrorism, raises confusing issues about the relationship between ethnic, religious, national, and international loyalties. For instance, students in the United States with Middle Eastern ties have been approached by U.S. government officials to answer queries, presumably about information they may have concerning current terrorist activities. The government's program to conduct interviews with such students has met with questions about constitutional rights and raised issues about linking a person's nationality with the person's political convictions. The same possible confusion between religious affiliation and political convictions has been a point of contention, especially when Muslims who are not proponents of terrorism nevertheless question U.S. integrity regarding the tapes of Osama bin Laden in which he speaks about his prior knowledge of the bombings. The drawing of a line in the sand has raised significant questions about international relationships, including the educational relationships among students, professors, and institutions, both in the United States and abroad.

Internationalizing Higher Education was in the making before 9/11, and the events of that fateful day will have repercussions for higher education. Thus, whenever it was deemed possible, authors of the chapters in this volume addressed potential repercussions of the 9/11 attack, such as likely policy changes in visa applications due to the linking of terrorism with particular countries. But 9/11 will not change many of the issues that the authors address, so readers can expect to find useful information that will help them as they pursue opportunities to internationalize their campus. Here is a preview of the chapters.

Chapter One, by Holly Moran Hansen, promotes the value of American students studying other cultures beginning in the American classroom and extending to study abroad programs.

Chapter Two, by Charles F. Abel, provides international students with research-based principles for being successful in the American classroom. Although the chapter is written for international students, professors will find Abel's strategies useful as they contemplate how to be effective teachers.

Chapter Three, by Jan Guidry Lacina, notes that campuses can improve their chances of retaining international students by providing students with help in adjusting to American higher education.

Chapter Four, by Arthur J. Sementelli, discusses ways that university administrators, professors, and students can run the visa gauntlet successfully. As Sementelli points out, obtaining a visa really is like running a gauntlet, but he provides details that will make the task easier than it would be otherwise.

Chapter Five, by Christina Murphy, Lory Hawkes, and Joe Law, explains the value of providing a Web-based orientation to international students. Their argument for Web-based orientation is compelling, especially given the widespread use of the Internet throughout the world.

Chapter Six, by David L. Sigsbee, is a cogent analysis of the failure in grades K–16 to provide adequate language training to students. But, as Sigsbee notes, American education does not need to continue its lackluster performance. Successful models of language training, even in our own country, provide educators with a blueprint for producing students who are fluent and proficient in at least one foreign language.

Chapter Seven, by Charles F. Abel and Arthur J. Sementelli, touches on the sticky problem of evaluating students' academic credentials, both for admission to programs and for transfer of credit.

Chapter Eight, by Samuel Fung and Joe Filippo, explains how professors teaching in the United States can become involved in study abroad and faculty exchange programs. When faculty members work in another country, they have the opportunity to enrich their teaching to promote greater cultural awareness when they return to teach in the United States.

Chapter Nine, by Patience A. Sowa, points out that student exchange programs are quite valuable, both to the U.S. economy and for students' intellectual development. Using a balanced approach, Sowa also points out the liabilities of such programs.

Chapter Ten, by Carolyn Davidson Abel, is written for international families who come to the United States for educational opportunities. Abel provides a great deal of practical advice about how families can adjust to American culture; in doing so, she lays out instructions that American professors and students can echo as they work with international families who are becoming acclimated to the United States.

Chapter Eleven, by Beth H. Carmical, provides a road map for initiating and developing international programs on campus. Her step-by-step approach is both thorough and practical.

Certainly, facets of international education will change, given the events of September 11, but the information authors have provided in this volume will continue to be valuable as individual professors and students, particular campus departments and units, and organizations throughout campus strive to provide opportunities for students, faculty, and administrators to learn more about the rich diversity of cultures throughout the world, to embrace people from those cultures, and to promote cultural diversity. In addition, the authors collectively have cataloged excellent strategies for helping international students become successful intellectually and socially during their stay in the United States. *Internationalizing Higher Education* is a full toolkit for those who want vital and growing international programs on their campuses.

Beth H. Carmical
Bruce W. Speck
Editors

BETH H. CARMICAL *is director of the Multi-Cultural Center and International Student Life at the University of North Carolina at Pembroke and serves as the FOCUS editor for the North Carolina Association of International Educators.*

BRUCE W. SPECK *is professor of English and vice president for academic affairs at Austin Peay State University in Clarksville, Tennessee. Previously, he was associate vice chancellor for academic affairs and dean of arts and sciences at the University of North Carolina at Pembroke. His work has appeared in a variety of professional journals.*

1

Professors and students can learn about other cultures by studying those cultures in the classroom, by participating in an exchange program, and by providing technical assistance to other cultures.

Defining International Education

Holly Moran Hansen

> International education is a dynamic concept that involves a journey or movement of people, minds, or ideas across political and cultural frontiers. The development of a "Worldmindedness" can become the goal of any school, and hence, any school can become truly "international."

Fraser and Brickman (Hayden and Thompson, 1995, p. 17), who described *international education* this way, perhaps encapsulated the most appropriate definition for a term that covers many areas and affects many people. Those of us in higher education are affected by international education in multiple ways. Whether a person studies overseas, teaches overseas, or interacts with people from a different country on a college campus in the United States, we are participants (consciously or unconsciously, physically or psychologically) in this "movement" to which Fraser and Brickman refer. What are the elements of this so-called movement? Arum (1987) divides international education into three parts: international studies, international educational exchange, and technical assistance. By examining each of these individual parts, we can take a closer look at where international education is today and what its future holds.

International Studies

Arum begins by identifying international studies as "all educational activities of any kind (i.e., teaching, studying, doing research or providing technical assistance), involving people of two or more nations, either individually or

I appreciate the insights and comments of Amy Jones and Evelyn Pierro on drafts of this chapter.

in formal programs" (p. 8). Because it is concrete and tangible, the classroom example is probably the most common type of international studies. Although it still does not compare to real-life experiences inside and outside the classroom, professors can add to the realism of the classroom. For example, my college French professor, in an attempt to go beyond a brief introduction to Reunion Island in the textbook, showed a film in French depicting a day in the life of a boy on the island. The film was followed by a comprehension check and discussion. This exercise introduced us to a new place where French is spoken, and it forced us to use our French to understand and participate in a discussion. However, it was still abstract. Because I had no personal connection to this place or to the boy depicted in the film, I remember very little of the information that was covered about the island.

However, I distinctly remember the French student who worked as an assistant in the French department in college and her visits to the classroom. Her name was Marie-Pierre and she was from Paris. She fascinated me because she was French. She was the first French person I had met. I observed her every move in the classroom and hung on to every French word she spoke. She liked Jacques Brel, a singer from Belgium who was famous in the 1950s in France. She played his music for us and explained the meaning of some of the lyrics. I had known I wanted to go to France before I met Marie-Pierre; meeting her reinforced my desire to go to France by bringing to life my ideas of how I had imagined France and French people to look and act. Thanks in part to her influence, the following year I went to France.

I have witnessed some much simpler examples of international studies outside the classroom. At the University of Northern Colorado (UNC), in Greeley, Colorado, where I work as a study abroad coordinator, I have seen students and faculty or staff connect on a daily basis. I have witnessed a student from India sharing a local dish with an administrative staff member for an afternoon snack. I have observed a Russian scholar explaining to an American student the details of an annual festival in her home country. For an American in the United States, these interactions easily spark an interest in the foreign country. Furthermore, the personal contact with people from other cultures forces Americans to react immediately, in real time. These meetings are more likely to have an impact in a personal way than if the same facts had been learned in a classroom.

International Educational Exchange

Arum then refers to international educational exchange as the subdivision of international education that "involves U.S. students and faculty studying, teaching and doing research abroad and foreign faculty and students studying, teaching and doing research in the U.S." (p. 13). To what end do these students and faculty members go overseas? As a study abroad coordinator, I hope that students will go abroad to learn, if nothing else, that there are differences between the host culture and that of the United States. These differences may range from religion to politics, from weather to food. One of my goals is to allow the students to experience these differences firsthand, away from the secure surroundings of their home country.

Ideally, American students will return from their study abroad proficient in the language spoken in the host country. Obvious reasons for this goal include being able to communicate on a daily basis while learning about the history and culture of the country; another is that students who can communicate on their own gain a great deal of independence and freedom in a foreign country. They are able to use public transportation, purchase items, and ask questions when they need to, all in the foreign language. With the barrier of the language aside, they experience less stress in their daily lives abroad. In addition to the independence, there is a sense of achievement that students will inevitably feel when they master the language used in their host culture.

Recently, I traveled to France to visit some of our students there on exchange. As I sat on the airplane in anticipation, I recalled how nervous I had been on my first trip to France as an exchange student more than ten years ago. My proficiency in French at that time was minimal. However, after one year I had conquered the language and felt a sense of ease when communicating. That sense of ease is still with me. During this recent trip, as I chatted casually with taxi drivers, communicated my needs to the staff at the hotel, and met with French administrators at the university, I still felt the sense of achievement. It was relaxing to know I wasn't going to experience more stress because I couldn't communicate. Gaining proficiency in the language has left me with a can-do attitude and an independence of which I am still proud—and will be for the rest of my life.

Finally, an important aspect to international exchange is the sense of identity one feels as a "foreigner" in a foreign country. Americans who are abroad can see America from the outside. This often causes them to make some keen observations about their home country that they would not have made had they never traveled abroad. American students who study abroad may find themselves defending or demystifying the stereotypes about America that are so prevalent in the media worldwide. Movies, music, and TV that promote violence cause misconceptions of what it's really like on a daily basis in a typical town in America. For example, I spent a considerable amount of time while living in Japan trying to convince Japanese people that I did not own a gun and had never been shot. At first I was offended by their questions and would tell them that such violence typically occurs *only* in large cities such as Los Angeles or New York (I am from a small town in the Midwest). Eventually, however, I realized that as an American, I am a representative of the big cities as well as the small towns, the good and bad aspects of our society. The fact that I was made uncomfortable by the stereotypes made me rethink my identity outside America and realize that it is different from my identity inside the country.

Technical Assistance

The final subdivision of international educational exchange, according to Arum, is technical assistance that "involves U.S. faculty and staff working to develop institutions and human resources abroad, primarily in Third World countries" (p. 18). He cites colleges and universities as the institutions with the highest number of technical assistance projects. Organizations such as the United Nations and the World Bank have a vested interest in these projects. The most popular field in which the technical assistance has taken place in the past has been the field of agriculture. He also mentions faculty exchanges in various departments where faculty members teach, study, and do research abroad. Ideally, the faculty member who returns from a stint abroad, in Arum's opinion, returns with a new sensitivity for both foreign and U.S.-based students. Arum mentions professors who have a personal interest in the field of international education.

For example, I recently met a professor at UNC who teaches information technology. He has proposed to carry out a technical assistance project on a much smaller scale than those done by the United Nations and the World Bank. He would like to see his students involved in a server project that would connect them with individuals from foreign countries. The reason he wants to promote this link between native and foreign students is not that he has studied abroad but that he had personal experience with international students when he was a college student. While he was attending a small college in the United States, this professor told me, he befriended students from China, Malaysia, and Singapore. He acted as their representative in the university town where they lived because these international students were repeatedly taken advantage of in their daily lives. They were overcharged at the grocery store and charged more for rent "just for being foreigners."

This professor, who had been raised in a homogenous American community, wanted to spend time with these students, partly because they were different from the people he had been exposed to growing up. Although he was intrigued by the fact that they spoke different languages and followed different cultural rules than he did, he also understood that they were human beings. As a fellow human being, he felt compelled to help them. As a result, friendships developed. He showed them how our culture works; in turn, they shared their cultures with him. Because of the strong bonds that were formed, this professor carries with him a sensitivity and compassion for international students. The impact these relationships had on him and the tough times he observed the international students experiencing, I believe, drove him to bring American and international students together for his server project. He is doing his part to contribute to international education. He will go to Italy and Poland next month, with his own money, to recruit students.

Effects of Internationalizing Higher Education

One of the driving forces behind the promotion of international education, undoubtedly, is the amount of money it brings to the U.S. economy. In 1999–2000, $12.3 billion was brought in (Schneider, 2000). In the university setting alone, extra revenue can be applied toward scholarships for American students to go abroad and can be used to hire more instructors to teach English as a second language to international students.

In the case of UNC, we hope to apply revenues and possible grant money toward the construction of a new international center of learning and cross-cultural exchange. One of our ideas is to have an Islamic center where Muslim students and their families can gather. Because we do not currently have a mosque or a cultural center for our Muslim students, most do not live in our town but in nearby communities where these gathering places are provided. Through sponsoring events and creating a meeting place for students to mingle and learn, this international center, we hope, will benefit the university as well as the surrounding community.

Above and beyond the international education and its impact on the economy and the university setting, though, there is a deeper and broader impact. Initiatives made on behalf of international education, according to King and Koller (1995), "have special importance to our local communities not only because they support current needs for our economic development, but also because they lay a foundation for the coming changes in the American workplace that will demand cross-cultural sensitivity and improved interpersonal skills" (p. 22). Because the awareness gained from a semester or year in a foreign country is not something tangible like money, it is more difficult for one to see its immediate impact. In the long run, however, it is highly possible that this awareness will be just as important as the revenue it brings.

To illustrate, in spite of the fact that computers have changed the ways in which we communicate and conduct our work, we in the industrialized world have realized that computers will never replace people. We will always need a person to repair the computer when it breaks down. In the same way, perhaps the future will show us that it is not so much technology and the Internet that will bring people together as nations. Instead, strengthening our relationship skills and finding commonalities among ourselves will be the best ways to communicate between nations. An observation made by one of our students currently studying in France drives this point home. She said she has learned that ultimately it's neither the technology nor the paperwork that matters most when trying to get things done in France. Rather, it's the one-on-one conversations and the development of relationships that count.

Present State of International Education

What is the current state of international education? How are we doing at U.S. colleges and universities when we look at each of the divisions Arum listed fourteen years ago? Raby (1998) explains that between 1988 and 1998, the number of international students at a consortium of fifty-four colleges in California increased from zero to fifty-three. Additionally, 26 percent of the fifty-four colleges (92 percent of the total in the consortium) refer to international education in their mission statement, and forty-eight of these colleges offer three or more foreign languages at their institutions. Although it is not clear how many of these schools offered foreign languages prior to 1988, currently the most commonly offered languages are Cantonese, French, German, Italian, Japanese, and Spanish. From these statistics, it is clear that the schools in this consortium have made an effort to expand their international student population, and, at the same time, to provide foreign language training for American students before they go abroad.

However, the number of U.S. students who study abroad for academic credit (129,770 in 1998–99) is extremely low when compared to approximately 514,000 foreign students at U.S. institutions and the approximately 15 million American students currently in higher education. Merryfield (1995) compares these statistics and points out that most Americans still go to Western Europe. Although there is nothing wrong with this, Merryfield suggests that "broadening the scope of exchanges and exchange participants will increase the range of experience and knowledge gained from study abroad" (p. 7). From personal experience, I can say that my year abroad in France while I was in college differed greatly from that of my experience teaching English on the Japan Exchange and Teaching Program. Not only were my objectives different when I was a working professional on exchange (compared to when I was a student) but the culture shock of Asia compared to Western Europe was considerably more difficult to work through. For instance, the three alphabets were completely different from the one I had learned in the United States and France. The customs, in some ways, were the opposite of those in the West. I learned that slurping one's soup or noodles is a compliment to the chef in Japan, whereas in the United States it is considered impolite. As a result of these differences, I feel that I overcame more obstacles to acclimate to the culture and language of Japan. At the same time, I took more from the experience in terms of self-knowledge and achievement. I learned how to be more patient with people when I was speaking English and not to take for granted they would understand me. I learned about the gratification of teaching people and seeing them make progress in English. Finally, I learned to be open-minded about cultural differences, even if I cannot understand all of them. By the end of my three years there, I felt as though I could reach any goal.

Merryfield goes on to suggest that American students should have more international education or study abroad opportunities before reaching the college level. Individuals working in the field of international education cannot expect students to express an interest in studying abroad if they have had little or no exposure to foreign cultures and people prior to beginning college. For example, some U.S. students have never crossed the border into a neighboring state. These students' perception of "foreign" could be a nearby state instead of a foreign country. Therefore, it is important to spark interest in and promote exposure to international education early on—to plant the seed, so to speak.

Young Americans need to know early on that there is a huge world outside the small one in which they live every day. Educators and parents can spark an interest in young people by introducing foreign cultures to them. They can talk about a day in the life of someone their age in a foreign culture. They can show Americans pictures and movies depicting the culture. Finally, the best way to spark an interest is by introducing the American youth to someone from a foreign culture. This is what will bring to life what they see in books and in movies; it will personalize the place and the culture and make it more real. Ideally, then, by the time students start college they have already begun thinking about studying abroad, if for no other reason initially than to visit their friend whom they met from a foreign country.

Conclusion

The current world events are important to international education in that they help us to see and, ideally, understand where patterns in cultural beliefs and behaviors come from. The attacks on September 11, 2001 affected the hearts of all Americans. Amazingly, as we watched those events unfold in the United States, we were touched to see so many nations sharing in our grief. This universality has shown the strength of our friendships with not only our allies but with nations who were considered to be enemies not long ago. We have seen evil, but we have also seen the good in people. We have proven our ability to work together, not only to overcome this evil but to continue our relationships with one another as individuals and nations. These individual relationships begin with international education. Mary Anne Grant, president and executive director of International Student Exchange Program (ISEP), said it best in an e-mail message (September 20, 2001) to ISEP members:

> The commitment of our community to peace, understanding and friendly relations among all nations and peoples has been reinforced as we respond to these terrible acts of aggression. International education and exchange helps to build understanding and tolerance of difference among peoples and cultures of the world. Now, more than ever, we must remain committed to our work and to supporting international students and scholars in the United States and abroad. ISEP joins our member institutions and colleague organizations in standing behind the value and importance of our endeavors.

Given this mind-set, more than ever we need to focus on cultivating relationships with other nations, to send students abroad to realize that other cultures and other ways of living exist besides our own. Finally, I hope that we continue to welcome students to our country, to share our culture, languages, and customs with them.

References

Arum, S. "International Education: What Is It? A Taxonomy of International Education of U.S. Universities." *CIEE Occasional Papers on International Educational Exchange,* 1987, *23,* 5–22.

Hayden, M., and Thompson, J. "International Education: The Crossing of Frontiers." *International Schools Journal,* 1995, Vol. XV, no. 1, 17. Originally published in Fraser, S. E., and Brickman, W. W. *A History of International and Comparative Education: Nineteenth Century Documents.* Glenview, Ill.: Scott Foresman, 1968.

King, M., and Koller, A. "Emerging Opportunities in International Education." *Community College Journal,* 1995, *65,* 20–25.

Merryfield, M. "Teacher Education in Global and International Education." *Eric Digest,* 1995.

Raby, R. L. *California Colleges for International Education (CCIE) 1997–1998 Annual Report.* 1998.

Schneider, M. "Others' Open Doors: How Other Nations Attract International Students: Implications for U.S. Educational Exchange." Syracuse University: Maxwell-Washington International Relations Semester and Summer Practicum, November 25, 2000.

HOLLY MORAN HANSEN *is a study abroad coordinator and international student adviser at the University of Northern Colorado in Greeley; she has lived in France and Japan.*

2

This chapter recommends strategies, based on current research into teaching and learning, that international students may use to improve their academic performance.

Academic Success and the International Student: Research and Recommendations

Charles F. Abel

As an international student, you may not realize that American education differs significantly from the education you are accustomed to in your country. Therefore, you may be interested in learning more about the ins and outs of the American classroom in higher education. This chapter provides you with research-based strategies for being successful in the American classroom.

Personal Practices and Academic Success

Empirically, effective learning by international students proves modestly related to language proficiency, learning strategies, study strategies, and certain personal characteristics. For example, the correlation between academic success and language proficiency, as measured by the Test of English as a Foreign Language (TOEFL), is low in magnitude but nevertheless positive and significant (Abadzi, 1984; Burgess and Greis, 1984; Heil and Aleamoni, 1974; Riggs, 1982). The TOEFL also correlates modestly but significantly with credits earned (Johnson, 1988; Light, Xu, and Mossop, 1987).

Empirical evidence also indicates that students who actively develop their own learning strategies and then actively organize and adjust their study behaviors prove significantly more successful than "passive learners" (Corno, 1986; Thomas and Rohwer, 1986; Weinstein and Mayer, 1986; Zimmerman, 1986). Similarly, academic success seems to correlate modestly with attitudes toward learning and learning strategies, as measured by the

Learning and Study Strategies Inventory (LASSI), an assessment measure of student-learning and test-taking strategies. Specifically, the number of course withdrawals by international students correlates significantly with LASSI scales that measure attitudes toward studying, effective time management, and concentration. The LASSI total score also correlates significantly with the number of withdrawals (Stoynoff, 1997). These findings and the literature commenting on them suggest some helpful steps for international students in developing an overall strategy for academic success.

Prepare for the American Educational Experience. The expectation in the United States is that students will demonstrate a good deal more individual initiative than is often expected in universities outside the United States (Baron, 1975). Some international students also expect more formal relationships with their professor than do most American students and so depend on professors to tell and do more for them than is expected in most American universities. Finally, international students may not be accustomed to the competitive environment of many American colleges and universities (Craig, 1981; Edwards and Tonkin, 1990). Preparing for the culture shock of a very different experience by auditing classes beforehand, visiting campus organizations, and speaking with American students about what to expect should prove helpful.

Determine the "Learning Time" Available for Each Course. A learning model developed by Carroll (1963) suggests that "learning time" and student perseverance are the most important variables in academic learning by international students. Available learning time depends on the calendar established by the university for each semester and the time allotted by professors for covering various topics in each class during the semester. International students should become thoroughly familiar with these constraints beforehand and should plan their study accordingly. Information on allotted learning time may be obtained by checking the university calendar either on the university Web site or in the catalogue. The catalogue is also a good place to find information on the amount of material a course will cover and a course's level of difficulty. Calendars may also be found in the "schedules of classes" published prior to each term by the university; it is a good idea to seek out the professor listed in the schedule as teaching the course you want to take. He or she may be able to give you a copy of the syllabus in advance and provide additional information on such items as how much material will be covered, what the required texts are, what sort of testing is involved (for example, objective or essay), and what additional course assignments are required (for example, term papers or projects).

Plan Your Study and Recreation Time. *Perseverance* refers to the student's intensity and focus on academic content during the allocated learning time. Carroll's study suggests that all else being equal, the more time you spend on a course and the better you focus on the material, the more successful you will be. Bolstering Carroll's model are findings by Moore

(1994) of a positive association between time management practices and academic success. This association is independent of aptitude, as predicted by scores on the Scholastic Aptitude Test (SAT). Similarly, Price (1996) found a significant positive relationship between time management and college grade point averages.

Begin managing your time by evaluating thoroughly how you spend it. The most important thing to consider is how you allot your study and recreation time. For most international students, studying for long, uninterrupted periods is most effective (Light, 2001). Devising ways of structuring such periods into your schedule will prove most beneficial.

Other tips for good time management include the following:

- Use a weekly calendar to plan your study and recreation.
- Plan two hours of study for each hour of class time.
- Plan to study during the day. Research shows that sixty minutes of study during the day is equivalent to ninety minutes of study at night (Pauk, 1989).
- Plan blocks of study time. Studying in one-hour blocks is usually best (Pauk, 1989).
- Have specific goals set for your study time and allot more than enough time to accomplish those goals.
- List your homework in order of importance. Tackle your most difficult homework first, and try to finish early so you'll have time to relax.
- Take breaks. Decide how long you will study before you take your first break, and decide how long your breaks will be.
- Schedule the time for reviewing your notes and readings every day.

Get the Right Kind of Peer Tutoring. Although McKeachie (1986) found that most peer tutoring was ineffectual, Trowbridge and others (1991) and Lidren, Meier, and Brigham (1991) found that small groups tutored by advanced undergraduates who supplemented lectures, readings, and projects were effective in improving test scores in certain subjects. The Office of Student Services can help you identify available tutors, and most universities have tutoring centers in their libraries. In addition, offices in the English, language, and math departments can direct you to writing, language, and math centers staffed by peer tutors.

Develop Visual Models of What You Are Learning. Gage and Berliner (1992) argue that models provide "accurate and useful representations of knowledge that is needed when solving problems in some particular domain" (p. 314). Specifically, they found that students who study models and conceptual maps before a lecture may recall as much as 57 percent more of the conceptual information than students who do not study and discuss such maps and models. For example, a visual model of this chapter might look like this:

Figure 2.1. Academic Success

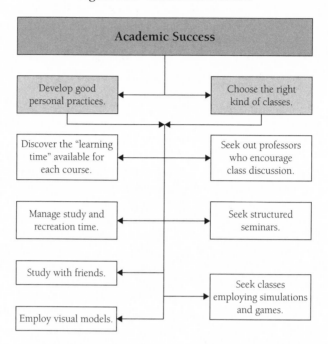

Join a Study Group and Discuss Study Material with Friends.
Zimmerman and Pons (1986) found higher academic achievement among
students who regularly used peers to help them learn. Boyer and Sedlacek
(1988) found that the strongest noncognitive predictor of international students' academic achievement was the support given by friends. They spec-
ulated that assistance from friends helped to overcome limitations in
language proficiency and cultural background.

What to Look for in Professors and Classrooms

Research findings by Eddy (1979), Stafford (1980), Wray (1981), and Craig
(1981) suggest that course structure and content are impediments to the academic success of international students in the United States. Research also
indicates that classroom atmosphere and especially the quality and degree of
faculty-student interaction in American universities trouble international students (Craig, 1981; Edwards and Tonkin, 1990). These findings reflect the
fact that most international students are accustomed to listening and learning rather than speaking in class. International students should therefore
consider seeking out professors who lecture well, and the advice that follows
is based on research into what constitutes effective lecturing techniques.

Information on which classes are lecture-oriented may be obtained
from university catalogues. Information on which professors employ which

techniques may be obtained from student evaluations. Many universities make student evaluations available in the library or through their Office of Student Services. Course syllabi obtained from the professor or from students having experience with particular professors is helpful as well. Along this line, "networking" with other students who enjoy a broad range of experience with professors across campus will provide detailed information on a professor's classroom techniques and general approach to learning. You might begin to identify student networks by obtaining a list of student organizations and events from the Office of Student Activities. This will provide information on meeting times and places. Look for groups and events with which you share interests, hobbies, or educational goals.

Seek Out Professors Who Encourage Class Participation. Although international students are inured to lecture formats, research indicates that after exposure to between ten and twenty minutes of continuous lecturing, learning falls off rapidly. Luckily, several teaching practices effectively counter this tendency. First, look for professors who ask rhetorical questions every ten minutes or so (Weaver and Cotrell, 1986) and who reinforce material by asking for nonthreatening forms of participation such as a show of hands or volunteer speakers with examples confirming or countering the material (Hunter, 1983). Finally, look for professors who catch attention and drive home their points through stories, metaphor, and myth. Experience indicates that the effective use of these devices increases attention to the material well beyond the otherwise operative ten- to twenty-minute time limit.

Research also indicates that enhanced understanding results when students discuss the meaning of what is presented in lectures. As international students tend to be more reticent than American students, you may counter this disadvantage by seeking out professors who provide models for participation by suggesting analyses or critiques of the lecture material (Frederick, 1987). Additionally, look for professors who present common experiences for discussion and employ visual and audio presentations. Common experiences establish personal connections with the content and provide shared referents for ideas. Visual and audio presentations provide a common experience, evoking different reactions and stimulating discussion. Case studies have a similar effect (Greenwood and Parkay, 1989).

Thought-provoking questions also invite participation, so look for professors who ask what interested, surprised, or shocked you, how you might do things differently or what you think might happen next. Good professors also follow up on your comments by requesting clarification and by helping you to refine or to rephrase your points in terms of the concepts and principles central to the content area.

Seek Out Structured Seminars. Although informal and less-structured classes are employed to stimulate engagement in American classrooms, the research mentioned earlier indicates that these practices may impede international student learning. In addition, international students are often unaccustomed to frequent testing and have more experience taking essay-oriented examinations. Several suggestions for coping with these impediments are suggested by the literature.

Learning theory suggests that essay-focused classes are most effective (Smilkstein, 1991). Look for classes requiring you to prepare short, out-of-class essays or "thought papers" on the reading or lecture material to be shared in class. This approach integrates a structured approach with active engagement and may prove quite comfortable to the international student as a transition into the American classroom. Alternatively, look for professors who solicit points of view, compile them, and ask the class to sift and refine them in pursuit of consensus. It is often helpful in these situations if the professor plays devil's advocate, drawing out points missed or too quickly dismissed by the class.

Seek Out Classes Employing Simulations and Games. Simulations and games suspend the normal classroom setting by creating an alternative reality, thereby changing students' behavioral expectations. International students may then be on a more equal footing with the rest of the class. Moreover, well-designed simulations and games may be more comfortable to international students, as they are necessarily well structured through rules, set goals, and structured relationships. Research indicates that such experiences with simulations and games may stimulate deeper insights into course content (Cloke, 1987).

Conclusion

Research indicates that academic success for the international student flows from the confluence of a number of factors, including language proficiency, learning strategies, and classroom dynamics. Equally important are the roles of social and educational assistance provided by study groups and peer tutoring. Carefully choosing professors and carefully monitoring the time spent on study, recreation, and "down time" are perhaps the most important strategies advancing academic success.

References

Abadzi, J. "Evaluation of Foreign Students' Admission Procedures Used at the University of Alabama." In G. Hale, C. Stansfield, and R. Duran (eds.), *Summaries of Studies Involving the Test of English as a Foreign Language, 1963–1982.* Princeton, N.J.: Educational Testing Service, 1984.

Baron, M. (ed.). *Advising, Counseling and Helping the Foreign Student.* Washington, D.C.: National Association for Foreign Student Affairs, 1975.

Boyer, S., and Sedlacek, W. "Noncognitive Predictors of Academic Success for International Students: A Longitudinal Study." *Journal of College Student Development,* 1988, *29,* 218–223.

Burgess, T., and Greis, N. "English Language Proficiency and Academic Achievement Among Students of English as a Second Language at the College Level." In G. Hale, C. Startsfield, and R. Duran (eds.), *Summaries of Studies Involving the Test of English as a Foreign Language, 1963–1982.* Princeton, N.J.: Educational Testing Service, 1984.

Carroll, J. "A Model for School Learning. *Teachers' College Record,* 1963, *64,* 723–733.

Cloke, P. "Applied Rural Geography and Planning: A Simple Gaming Technique." *Journal of Geography in Higher Education,* 1987, *11*(1), 35–45.

Corno, L. "The Metacognitive Control Components of Self-Regulated Learning." *Contemporary Educational Psychology,* 1986, *11,* 333–336.

Craig, B. L. "Variations and Themes in International Education." *Educational Record,* 1981, *62,* 41–46.

Eddy, M. S. "Foreign Students in the United States: Is the Welcome Mat Out?" *AAHE-ERIC Higher Education Currents,* 1979. (ED 165525)

Edwards, J., and Tonkin, H. (eds.). *Internationalizing the Community College: Strategies for the Classroom.* New Directions for Community Colleges, no. 70. San Francisco: Jossey-Bass, 1990.

Frederick, P. J. "Student Involvement: Active Learning in Large Classes." In M. G. Weimer (ed.), *Teaching Large Classes Well.* New Directions for Teaching and Learning, no. 32. San Francisco: Jossey-Bass, 1987.

Gage, N., and Berliner, D. *Educational Psychology.* (5th ed.) Boston: Houghton Mifflin, 1992.

Greenwood G., and Parkay, F. *Case Studies for Teacher Decision Making.* New York: Random House, 1989.

Heil, D., and Aleamoni, L. "Assessment of the Proficiency in the Use and Understanding of English by Foreign Students as Measured by the Test of English as a Foreign Language." In G. Hale, C. Standsfield, and R. Duran (eds.), *Summaries of Studies Involving the Test of English as a Foreign Language, 1963–1982.* Princeton, N.J.: Educational Testing Service, 1974.

Hunter, M. *Reinforcement.* El Segundo, Calif.: Tip Publications, 1983.

Johnson, P. "English Language Proficiency and Academic Performance of Undergraduate International Students." *TESOL Quarterly,* 1988, *22,* 164–168.

Lidren, D., Meier, S., and Brigham, T. "The Effects of Minimal and Maximal Peer Tutoring Systems on the Academic Performance of College Students." *Psychological Record,* 1991, *41*(1), 69–78.

Light, R. *Making the Most of College: Students Speak Their Minds.* Cambridge, Mass.: Harvard University Press, 2001.

Light, R., Xu, M., and Mossop, J. "English Proficiency and Academic Performance of International Students." *TESOL Quarterly,* 1987, *21,* 251–260.

McKeachie, W. *Teaching Tips: A Guidebook for the Beginning College Teacher.* (8th ed.) Lexington, Mass.: D.C. Heath, 1986.

Moore, P. "The Influence of Time Management Practices and Perceptions on Academic Performance." *Dissertation Abstracts International,* 1994, *55*(7-B), 3051.

Pauk, W. *How to Study in College.* (2nd ed.) Boston: Houghton Mifflin, 1989.

Price, D. "The Relationship of Self-Management, Time-Management, and Personality Measurements to Academic Performance." *Dissertation Abstracts International,* 1996, *57*(7-A), 2860.

Riggs, J. "Cloze Testing Procedures in ESL: A Prediction of Academic Success of Foreign Students and a Comparison with TOEFL Scores." In G. Hale, C. Stansfield, and R. Duran (eds.), *Summaries of Studies Involving the Test of English as a Foreign Language, 1963–1982.* Princeton, N.J.: Educational Testing Service, 1982.

Smilkstein, R. "A Natural Teaching Method Based on Learning Theory." *A Forum for Teachers and Learners.* Seattle: Seattle Community Colleges, 1991.

Stafford, T. "Adjustment of International Students." *NASPA Journal,* 1980, *18*(1), 40–45.

Stoynoff, S. "Factors Associated with International Students' Academic Achievement." *Journal of Instructional Psychology,* 1997, *24,* 56–69.

Thomas, J., and Rohwer, W. "Academic Studying: The Role of Learning Strategies." *Educational Psychologist,* 1986, *21,* 19–41.

Trowbridge, N. Unpublished manuscript cited in D. Lidren, S. Meier, and T. Brigham, "The Effects of Minimal and Maximal Peer Tutoring Systems on the Academic Performance of College Students. *Psychological Record,* 1991, *41*(1), 69.

Weaver, R., and Cotrell, H. "Using Interactive Images in the Lecture Hall." *Educational Horizons*, 1986, *64*(4), 180–185.

Weinstein, C. E., and Mayer, R. E. "The Teaching of Learning Strategies." In M. C. Wittrock (ed.), *Handbook of Research on Teaching*. New York: Macmillan, 1986.

Wray, H. "Abroad in the U.S.: Foreign Students on American Campuses." *Educational Record*, 1981, *62*(3), 68–71.

Zimmerman, B. J. "Becoming a Self-Regulated Learner: Which Are the Key Sub-Processes? *Contemporary Educational Psychology*, 1986, *11*, 307–313.

Zimmerman, B. J., and Pons, M. M. "Development of a Structured Interview for Assessing Student Use of Self-Regulated Learning Strategies." *American Educational Research Journal*, 1986, *23*(4), 614–628.

CHARLES F. ABEL is assistant professor of political science and director of The Knowledge Factory, a center for basic and applied research at Stephen F. Austin State University in Nacogdoches, Texas.

3

This chapter highlights what research says about the social successes and challenges international students face in college.

Preparing International Students for a Successful Social Experience in Higher Education

Jan Guidry Lacina

International students' interactions with other people (their social life) form an integral part of their college experience in the United States. Often they have problems adjusting to their new environment. Some students experience loneliness; others may have problems due to their unfamiliarity with U.S. customs and values. International students may also experience a loss of social status because their social standing in their homeland may not be recognized as important in the United States (Al-Sharideh and Goe, 1998). This chapter presents a discussion of the social challenges that international students face when leaving their homeland for school in the United States and highlights ways colleges and universities can encourage the social success of international students.

Adjusting to American Universities

International students tend to share certain characteristics, despite their diverse cultural, social, religious, and political backgrounds (Thomas and Althens, 1989). Unlike immigrants, international students are usually in the United States for only a short period of time. As a result, they are a group in transition for the purpose of achieving an educational goal (Sakurako, 2000). Because their families and social networks are left behind in their home countries, international students are forced to form new social networks. And these networks are often very different from the traditional college students' social support system, as the traditional student may have a family living in the same state. Overall, international students have very different backgrounds from their American peers, and these differences often lead to discrimination.

Language Diversity. Language discrimination hinders many international students from adapting to a new social environment. Even though the United States has a long history of bilingualism, Americans remain xenophobic (Crawford, 2000; Lessow-Hurley, 2000). Many Americans do not have the patience to listen to someone whose accent is different from their own, or they are fearful of other cultures or nationalities due to stereotypes they have of different groups (Crawford, 2000). Overall, the United States tends to be linguistically unsophisticated and maintains a parochial attitude toward multilingualism (Crawford, 2000; Lessow-Hurley, 2000). The English Only Movement exemplifies how Americans view multilingualism or bilingualism. For example, Crawford (2000) posits that many supporters of the English Only Movement believe that language diversity often leads to language conflict or ethnic hostility. As a result, diplomacy and international relations have suffered, and many international students do not feel welcomed by Americans. This will most likely continue, given the recent terrorist attacks on the World Trade Center and the Pentagon.

An international student's accent or use of different expressions can interfere with communication while he or she is conversing with an American. For international students to be well prepared for social interaction, they need to be familiar with idioms and college slang, as well as proficient in academic English (see Chapter Two). Many international students acquire academic English so they can function successfully in their college classrooms but have little acquaintance with the language used in social situations. For example, an American university student might say "Get out of here," which literally means "leave." However, a speaker might use this phrase figuratively when he or she is merely joking. Likewise, statements such as "Let's get together" and "I'll call you soon" are often misinterpreted by international students (Sakurako, 2000). For many American students, these statements are just a polite way of ending a conversation; miscommunication often results when the international student interprets the statements literally. University faculty or college peers who use these idioms need to explain their meaning to international students.

Cultural Differences. Cultural differences may also play a role in the international students' ability or inability to form social relationships. The concept of friendship is often viewed differently in diverse cultures. For example, Bulthuis (1986) states that, because America is a highly individual-oriented society, friendship is sometimes viewed as less permanent than in other cultures. International students may notice when they first arrive on campus that everyone appears to be friendly to everyone else. People may smile and say hello and ask such questions as "How are you?" But that question is meant as a statement rather than a question. And it may appear odd to the international student when the speaker does not wait for an answer, thus seeming rude or insincere. After the international student has interacted with American students, the American students may begin to seem more interested in superficial socializing than in becoming close or trusted friends.

Problems may also arise when students misinterpret the translation of a word or a phrase. Spinks and Wells (1997) use the phrase "cool dude" as an example. This phrase to the American college student means the same as "OK," but for international students it may mean something entirely different. They may think the speaker is referring to someone's body temperature being below normal. Another example is that Americans who refer to "taking a bus" do not mean "stealing a bus." Spinks and Wells (1997) tell the story of a man from a different culture who was told to "run across town" to a CPA firm to bring back a folder. Unfortunately, he misunderstood the phrase "run across town," and he literally ran the distance to pick up his folder. University faculty must choose their words carefully when interacting with international students, and international students must likewise become familiar with everyday phrases spoken in the United States to prevent miscommunication.

Dave's ESL Café [http://www.eslcafe.com/] is a good place for international students to begin learning new idioms and slang to better understand informal English and a good place for college faculty to become familiar with ESL (English as a Second Language) issues. This site offers numerous discussion boards that are applicable for both administrators and professors to use, such as "English for Specific Purposes," "Business English," and "Making Friends."

Misunderstanding can also exist when an American from the opposite sex makes statements such as "Let's get together sometime" or "Stop by my place." Pedersen (1991) asserts that friendly statements by Americans are often misinterpreted by international students as romantic invitations. As a result, some international students may be left confused and frustrated by cross-cultural communication. In like manner, men from countries that openly discriminate against women may find it difficult to accept women as their equals. The role of women in society in many countries resembles the role that women played at the turn of the century in the United States. It may be especially difficult for those men who have been segregated in all-male schools to respect U.S. female professors as authority figures in an academic field. After experiencing many problems with cross-cultural communication and discrimination, international students can become discouraged from seeking friendship with Americans (Bulthuis, 1986; Sakurako, 2000).

In like manner, religion is an important element to consider when discussing cultural differences. There appears to be no greater influence on cultural customs and practices than religion. And most people from diverse cultures throughout the world tend to view their religion as right and feel great social pressures when they believe their religious beliefs have been violated (Spinks and Wells, 1997). In the United States, many Americans are unreceptive to religions other than Christianity. This can become an issue when international students belong to non-Christian religious groups and, in particular, when they need to miss class to attend religious meetings. For example, during certain holy days, Muslims may need to attend prayers at the mosque, or they may need to fast for a number of days. Students who are fasting may experience a time in which they are tired or drowsy during class and may not participate as readily. University faculty should seek to accept diverse religions and customs and to be flexible when students need to attend religious events if they want to attract and retain international students.

Cross-Cultural Counseling

Crisis situations may develop for the international student as a result of the transition to a new culture and social environment (Sakurako, 2000). For example, international students may experience extreme loneliness and culture shock or physical symptoms such as headaches, insomnia, mental exhaustion, and many other symptoms due to stress caused by adjustment to a new culture. Adjusting to American roommates and trying to find friends eventually causes excessive stress on some students. Overall, international students experience more problems in college than American students do (Pedersen, 1991). However, studies suggest that even though many international students are very much in need of psychological help, mental health services are generally underused by these students. Those few international students who actually seek mental health assistance while in college are more likely than their American peers to terminate this service prematurely (Bradley and others, 1995; Pedersen, 1991).

The termination of mental health services is a result of many misunderstandings about the mental health field. For example, international students may view those who seek psychological help as dishonorable to their family, or they may be suspicious of the counselors. International students are under great stress to do well academically in this country because of the large amounts of money provided to them by either their families or their government. Similarly, international students may be wary of the counselors because many counselors are from the mainstream Euro-American culture, and international students may be suspicious of a counselor's motives for helping a student of a different color or nationality (Sakurako, 2000). Some students who are supported by their government to attend school in the United States may also be fearful that their appointments with the counselors might be reported to their government officials; as a result, they are scared that they may be asked to return to their homeland. This would only result in great shame to the student and to his or her family.

Encouraging a Positive Social Experience

Universities can employ various ways to encourage international students to develop a positive social experience while enrolled in a U.S. university. The first way a university can help the student is by providing an international student center with advisers and counselors who can help students with common problems such as culture, social life, health care, money matters, and so on. An international center can also be helpful in organizing social events; international students can meet other international students and American students as well.

Numerous international student centers throughout the United States help students develop a positive social life. For example, the University of California at Los Angeles [http://www.saonet.ucla.edu/intl/DISC/default.htm] holds a Welcome Dance when students arrive on campus. Each semester, all new international students (about 450 in all) are invited to attend this dance to meet other students and the international student center staff. The semiformal dance is catered, and the students are able to meet center volunteers and students from many different countries.

San Diego State University (SDSU) also welcomes new international students to its campus but does it through an e-mail exchange called the Email Partners Program [http://www.sa.sdsu.edu/isc/emailpartners.htm]. The program matches incoming SDSU students with student volunteers who have been at SDSU for a semester or more. The e-mail mentors help answer questions about adjusting to life in the United States, and they can provide advice on housing, academic classes, transportation, shopping, and friends.

Many universities with large international student populations have conversational group meetings scheduled by the international student center. When a program is large enough, it can offer conversation groups for a variety of purposes, such as having academic conversations, practicing for the SPEAK (Speaking Proficiency English Assessment Kit) test, and practicing social conversations with American students. The University of California at Los Angeles offers a Web site describing their conversational groups [http://www.saonet.ucla.edu/intl/DISC/default.htm]. The University of Kansas' Applied English Center (AEC) [http://www.aec.ukans.edu/Recruit/iss.html] also offers such conversational groups. These are free to any international student and are composed of three to four international students who are paired with an American student.

International movie clubs can help promote friendships among international students and other college students. Most universities that offer such a club tend to promote awareness of quality films from around the world and offer the international and the local community an inexpensive opportunity to have fun. Many universities offer these movies for free and provide popcorn and drinks. UCLA has a Web page for their international movie club, which gives information about movies that are playing each week [http://www.saonet.ucla.edu/intl/DISC/default.htm].

Other university campuses house a variety of individual student organizations for international students. For example, the University of Kansas houses about thirty diverse groups [http://www.aec.ukans.edu/Recruit/Groups.html].

The Muslim Association [http://www.ukans.edu/%7Emsa/] is one example of such a student group. This group's goals are to (1) promote unity and joint action among Muslims; (2) conduct social, cultural, religious, and other activities in the best traditions of Islam; (3) arrange and hold congregational prayers and Islamic religious festivals at appropriate times; (4) promote friendly relations between Muslims and non-Muslims; and (5) endeavor to make Islamic teachings known to interested non-Muslims. The University of Kansas represents a midwestern university that serves a wide variety of international students with vastly different religious and cultural backgrounds. By providing and encouraging such groups on campus, students are able to make friends who have backgrounds similar to theirs and, in the long run, to experience a more positive university social experience.

Conclusion

Most U.S. universities have a great need to increase student enrollment; as a result, they often try to attract international students. Such students are attractive because they are required to pay high out-of-state tuition and are viewed as serious, dedicated students. If we want to attract and retain international students on our university campuses, we must focus on the students' needs and successes in the American university experience. The social environment is one important aspect of the university experience that should not be ignored by university faculty. University administrators and professors need to be aware of the problems many international students face in adjusting to the United States and of the ways that administration and faculty can help students adjust. Likewise, university campuses that wish to retain their international students need to plan activities that encourage social interaction between the international students and American university students. When universities acknowledge the importance of the international students' social environment, both groups win—enrollment climbs and international students are happy.

References

Al-Sharideh, K. A., and Goe, W. R. "Ethnic Communities Within the University: An Examination of International Students." *Research in Higher Education*, 1998, 39(6), 699–725.

Bradley, L., Parr, G., Lan, W. Y., Bingi, R., and Gould, L. J. "Counseling Expectations of International Students." *International Journal for the Advancement of Counseling*, 1995, 18, 21–31.

Bulthuis, P. (ed.). *The Foreign Student Today: A Profile.* New Directions for Student Services, no. 3. San Francisco: Jossey-Bass, 1986.

Crawford, J. *At War with Diversity: US Language Policy in an Age of Anxiety.* New York: Multilingual Matters, 2000.

Lessow-Hurley, J. *The Foundations of Dual Language Instruction.* New York: Longman, 2000.

Pedersen, P. B. "Counseling International Students." *Counseling Psychologist,* 1991, *19,* 10–58.

Sakurako, M. "Addressing the Mental Health Concerns of International Students." *Journal of Counseling and Development,* 2000, 78(2), 137–144.

Spinks, N., and Wells, B. "Intercultural Communication: A Key Element in Global Strategies." *Career Development International,* 1997, 2(6), 287–292.

Thomas, K., and Althens, G. "Counseling Foreign Students." In P. B. Pedersen, J. G. Draguns, W. J. Lonner, and J. E. Trimble (eds.), *Counseling Across Cultures.* (3rd ed.) Honolulu: University of Hawaii, 1989.

JAN GUIDRY LACINA is an assistant professor in the Department of Elementary Education at Stephen F. Austin State University. She received her Ph.D. in curriculum and instruction/TESOL from the University of Kansas (1999). She is the author of numerous articles in the areas of ESL and teacher education.

4

This chapter illustrates current challenges for obtaining a visa, explains the legal processes, addresses issues associated with family members who also desire residence, and provides a set of strategies to use as a checklist throughout the process.

Running the Visa Gauntlet

Arthur J. Sementelli

As this chapter demonstrates, obtaining a U.S. visa is a complex process. To help students, potential non-native university employees, and institutions of higher education understand the visa gauntlet, I provide information about types of visas and strategies for obtaining a visa.

Advice for Students

Full-time students should obtain either an F-1 or an M-1 visa; spouses and children of F-1 or M-1 visa holders should obtain an F-2 or M-2 visa. F-class visas are designed for students engaging in a full course of academic study; M-class visas are typically used for vocational or technical training. Students can apply for "exchange visitor" status, allowing them to obtain a J-1 visa, which allows foreign nationals to come to the United States temporarily for consultation, training, research, or teaching. If you enter the United States with an F-class visa, you may change to an M-class visa if you transfer to a technical school.

The next challenge for full-time students is to get the proper forms. When you are admitted to a college or university for full-time study, the school should send you an I-20 form, which is the application for an F-1 visa. If you intend to be an exchange visitor, the agency or organization sponsoring you should send an IAP-66 form, which allows you to apply for a J-1 visa. In some cases, if you study English before entering a college or university, your government and the U.S. Embassy or U.S. Consulate may require a "conditional acceptance" from the college or university you ultimately wish to attend. This letter will promise you admission later if you satisfactorily complete an English language course.

After successful completion of the course, you will need to get an I-20 form from your English language institute. In addition, you must demonstrate that you have financial support for the entire time you plan to study in the United States. Get an "Affidavit of Support" form from the U.S. Embassy or U.S. Consulate. Complete this form with information about your sources of financing, and submit it along with your other documents. Typically, you must prove you are in good health. Check with the U.S. Embassy or U.S. Consulate to find out if such proof is necessary when traveling from your country.

You should also get to the right places to ensure your forms are processed correctly. After you have received your I-20 form or IAP-66 form, take the form along with your passport to a U.S. Embassy or consular official in charge of nonimmigrant visas. Once you complete your studies, if you have an F or M visa, you must leave the United States, get permission for practical training, or apply for a different type of visa. If you have had an F-1 visa for nine months, you may apply to stay in the United States for up to one year for practical training directly related to your field of study. If you are an "exchange visitor" who has come to the United States to be trained in a program not available in your home country, you may be permitted to stay for this training for up to eighteen months after you finish your studies if your sponsor approves this training. Exchange visitors (J-1) must return home for at least two years after finishing their program of study.

Advice for Faculty

International faculty will experience similar challenges to their student counterparts. The first step is to pick the right visa for your needs. Beyond that, potential employees should establish a good working relationship with the organization they intend to work in. Obtaining a visa for faculty requires quite a bit of coordination between the applicant and sponsoring organization. In addition, some visas require an Employment Authorization Document (EAD). The EAD is the primary method of determining whether you can work in the United States. The EAD paperwork must be renewed six months before it runs out and can be replaced if lost or stolen. Current policies for EAD approval allow non-native workers to be issued an interim EAD if ninety days have elapsed since their application was submitted. Please refer to the INA 247A document and the code of federal regulations 8 CFR 274a for more details about employer and employee responsibilities. This information can be accessed from the INS Web site [http://www.ins .usdoj.gov].

One popular option for faculty is the H1-B visa. The H1-B classification applies to persons in an occupation that requires the use of highly specialized knowledge. This option requires a "labor attestation" issued by the U.S. Secretary of Labor and is sought by the computing industry, the U.S.

Department of Defense, and others. Roughly 195,000 of these visas are currently approved. Current legislation indicates that this cap will be reduced to roughly 65,000 by 2003 if no further actions are taken. The limited access to this type of visa, combined with relatively tight competition among corporations, often forces universities to seek other options.

To obtain the H1-B visa, employers need to demonstrate that the applicant possesses specific expertise by a combination of work experience and education. The general rule is that three years of progressive experience can substitute for one year of education. Credentials obtained in foreign countries are screened for U.S. equivalency. Once finished with these steps, the potential employee can apply for an H1-B visa, which is valid for three years and can be renewed for an additional three years.

To get an H1-B visa, the employer must first send applications to the U.S. Department of Labor and the INS. Second, the employer must realize that the three-year limit can be renewed only once for an additional three years. No exceptions are made to this six-year limit. The process can take ten weeks to approve and can be complicated if the professional status of an applicant is unclear.

Another choice is the O-1 visa, which is designed for non-native workers with "extraordinary ability." In the case of higher education, this would be useful for attracting a "premier" scholar. The onus is on the applicant and sponsoring body to demonstrate how the applicant warrants such a classification. The O-1 has not received the media attention that the H1-B has, providing the additional benefits of being less well known and not requiring an EAD. However, no one who enters the United States under an O-1 visa can receive compensation from anyone other than the sponsoring body.

To obtain an O-1 visa, employers must (1) file an I-129 application with an O supplement and (2) demonstrate an applicant's extraordinary ability, with written support from peers and professional organizations. The visa is valid for three years and can be renewed by an unlimited number of one-year extensions. Applicants must file the O-2 documentation separately for dependents; if the deadline lapses, applicants have a relatively short cushion of time (about ten days) in which to reapply.

A third choice for faculty is the J-1 visa, which has institutional requirements for sponsors. They must have adequate funding, sponsor a minimum of five candidates annually, ensure that the time of service lasts a minimum of three weeks, and have an identifiable officer who is responsible for administering the exchange program on-site. Otherwise, applicants would follow the same basic steps as students applying for the J-1.

To obtain the J-1 visa, employers must first file the IAP–66 form. Throughout the process, employers and employees must be aware of the ending date for their status (not the visa expiration date), in case the university extends the employment contract. In addition, employers should both ensure that the employee's passport remains up-to-date and that the employee does not accept unauthorized employment. Finally, always make sure the employee meets USIA health requirements.

The Influence of NAFTA

Changes in NAFTA (North American Free Trade Agreement) have created options for nationals in Canada and Mexico. They can apply for a TN visa. "TN" is a special designation for NAFTA visas that are called Free Trade Professional visas. The Mexican applicants must possess at a minimum a licenciatura degree, and their Canadian counterparts must possess a Canadian bachelor's degree and fall within the guidelines established in Schedule 2 of the agreement (North American Free Trade Agreement, 1993, Chapter 10). Most higher education employees should be qualified for either the TN-1 (Canadian) or TN-2 (Mexican) options. The TN-class visas are granted for one year but can be renewed indefinitely, making them more flexible than the H-, O-, or J-class visas. In addition, they can be obtained at the border rather than through couriers and are often easier to get than other visas, especially the H1-B. The TN visas give the option of applying for permanent residency if an applicant so desires, making this useful for employers who wish to hire Canadian or Mexican nationals permanently.

A final option is the "permanent residence program," which is conceptually similar to the H1-B process except that the employee can stay in the United States for life (West and Bogumil, 2000). The drawbacks for this option are (1) it can take roughly three years to complete, (2) the paperwork is much more extensive than other visa options, and (3) the number of people who can obtain these visas is limited. The permanent residence program requires a long-term commitment from employers and is often not feasible, based on the numbers that are granted each year (about 17,000 for second preference and 42,000 for third preference).

Eligibility of Dependents

Employers must also address concerns about dependents. Each visa listed earlier has a corresponding dependent classification. The easiest approach for administrators is to file the comparable set of forms for dependents at the same time they file forms for their potential employees. In each case, the employer must realize the nuances associated with each possible visa, mostly regarding limitations on spousal work privileges. Always consult the most current updates to INS publications first, and talk to an INS official if this is your first time hiring a non-native employee; current regulations are often in flux.

The H1-B and H2-B counterpart is the H-4. No dependent granted an H-4 visa can be employed or receive compensation in the United States, making it difficult when employing couples who both have professional skills.

The O-3 has a similar clause. The TN visa allows spouses and children to enter the United States without an application fee, but dependents cannot work under any circumstances. If employers are careful and the employee's spouse is skilled, they can apply for a different visa for the spouse (H1-B, J-1, O-1, TN-1).

The "J" designation of visas is more flexible toward dependents than either the O-1 or the H classifications. The J-2 visa allows dependents of the J-1 visa to work, with INS permission. The dependent must be issued an EAD but may work for any employer. The employer must also verify authorization to work for each dependent and be aware of the EAD expiration dates.

General Eligibility

Some people are not eligible for a U.S. visa. The current laws provide for three major ways to deny entry. The first is health-based. Anyone who (1) has a communicable disease that is a threat to U.S. citizens, (2) has a disorder—mental or physical—that could threaten the property, safety, or welfare of him- or herself or others, (3) is a possible recurring threat to the property, safety, or welfare of him- or herself or others, or (4) is a drug abuser is not eligible. The second way excludes criminals, including those who (1) have a record of violations of state laws under the controlled substances act, (2) are characterized as possessing moral turpitude, (3) have multiple criminal convictions, (4) have been convicted of prostitution and commercialized vice, or (5) are aliens involved in serious crimes and immune from prosecution. The third way is security-related, including people who are (1) involved in espionage, (2) engaged in terrorist activities, or (3) are current members of the Palestine Liberation Organization. The information I have just provided is drawn from the 1990 Immigration and Nationality Act and could be subject to change. Employers who have questions about employee backgrounds should check with the INS for possible exemptions as early as possible in the effort to obtain a visa.

Strategies for Running the Visa Gauntlet

Employing non-native workers can be a useful way to address current staffing problems at universities, especially in technical fields. A few strategies can help make this somewhat complex process a bit easier. The following section will present some ideas for potential students, faculty, and organizations to use as guidelines when considering non-native employees.

Universities need to think about staffing decisions strategically. They must assign people and establish policies to deal with the process. First, consult with an immigration attorney (and not simply university legal counsel, who is typically a generalist) to determine what the current U.S. policies are for temporary residents in the United States. Second, establish an identifiable person in the HR Department to act as program officer (especially for the J-type visas). Third, develop a plan to determine what percentage of the overall staff is likely to be made up of non-native people and determine whether to adopt an institutional or contractual solution. Fourth, get access to the forms listed earlier (including the IAP-66 and EAD forms). Preparation in these four areas should help reduce problems associated with obtaining a visa.

Once a university has decided to pursue the employment of non-native persons, additional items must be considered. First, determine whether a non-native person is eligible for employment by contacting the INS Visa Services Public Inquiries branch. INS policies change with political, military, and economic shifts. If the person is ineligible, it is best to know early in the process before university funds are spent. Second, target the visa desired, realizing that this step will determine the time and paperwork involved in the process. It might be quick and simple (if you seek the TN class visa) or complex (if you choose the permanent resident program). In addition, you should inquire about dependents, current quota levels, and access when contacting the INS. Finally, you should establish a time line that is consistent with the type of visa being sought. Build a two-month period to work through an H1-B visa, for example, and communicate regularly with your program officer and INS representative. Finally, remember that there are avenues for changing visa status once your employee has arrived in the United States.

Conclusion

This chapter has presented an overview for navigating through the processes for obtaining a variety of U.S. visas. Please be aware that this treatment is necessarily brief and should not be substituted for the advice of appropriate governmental agencies or experienced legal counsel with a specialization in immigration law. Realizing these limitations, universities have multiple options for satisfying their staffing requirements outside the highly competitive H1-B visa. If you are hiring from a country that is part of NAFTA, the process should be rather simple. However, a few aspects of these processes (such as dealing with dependents) could unnecessarily complicate matters if they are not addressed in a timely way. To provide you with additional resources for learning about the visa gauntlet, I include a suggested reading list.

Suggested Reading

Arnold, D., and Niederman, F. "The Global IT Work Force (Company Business and Marketing)." *Communications of the ACM,* 2001, 7(44), 30–33.

Congress Daily A.M. "INS Reports Increasing Fraud Among H1-B Applicants (Immigration and Naturalization Service)." *National Journal Inc.,* 1999, 1.

Cronin, M. Testimony of Michael Cronin: Acting Associate Commissioner for Programs Immigration and Naturalization Service before the House Judiciary Committee

Subcommittee on Immigration and Claims Regarding Visa Waiver Pilot Program. Rayburn House Office Building, Room 2226, February 10, 2000.

Ellis, M., and Wright, R. "When Immigrants Are Not Migrants: Counting Arrivals of the Foreign Born Using the U.S. Census." *International Migration Review*, 1998, *1*(32), 127–144.

Glanz, J. "Proposals That Would Limit Visas Strike Fear at Universities." *Science*, 1996, *5259*(272), 190–191.

Immigration and Nationality Act, 8 U.S.C. 1001, *et seq.*, as amended by Public Law 101–549, Washington, D.C., 1990.

Johnson, J., Farrell, W., and Guinn, C. "Immigration Reform and the Browning of America: Tensions, Conflicts and Community Instability in Metropolitan Los Angeles." *International Migration Review*, 1997, *4*(31), 1055–1095.

Martin, P. "Mexican–U.S. Migration: Policies and Economic Impacts." *Challenge* (Mar.-Apr., 1995), 56–62.

Office of International Students and Scholars. *Visa and Immigration Information*. New Haven, Conn.: Yale University, 2000.

U.S. Department of Immigration and Naturalization. *Naturalization Guide*. Washington, D.C.: U.S. Department of Justice, 1999.

U.S. Department of Immigration and Naturalization. *Handbook for Employers (M-274)*. Washington D.C.: U.S. Department of Justice, 1991.

U.S. Immigration and Naturalization Service, Office of Inspections. *North American Free Trade Agreement NAFTA Handbook*. Washington, D.C.: U.S. Department of Justice, 1999.

References

The North American Free Trade Agreement. Washington, D.C.: U.S. Government Printing Office, 1993.

West, L., and Bogumil, W. "Foreign Knowledge Workers as a Strategic Staffing Option." *Academy of Management Executive*, 2000, *4*(14), 71–83.

ARTHUR J. SEMENTELLI coordinates the undergraduate public administration program at Stephen F. Austin State University in Nacogdoches, Texas.

5

Web-based orientation programs can be particularly effective means of responding to the academic, social, personal, and financial needs of international students and helping them prepare to enter into their new intercultural educational experiences.

How International Students Can Benefit from a Web-Based College Orientation

Christina Murphy, Lory Hawkes, Joe Law

The difficulties in the transition to college or graduate school that most students face are magnified for international students. In addition to the typical problems associated with any new change in direction or location, international students must deal with feelings of dislocation, adjustments to new cultures, and long-term, geographically vast separations from home and family. Often, differences in languages and social mores come into play as well.

Colleges and universities recognize the need to ease the transition for students and work extensively on developing orientation programs that will acquaint students with the campus and the community. The use of the Web for such orientation programs is widely acknowledged in providing information to noninternational students and parents alike. What is less clear for many colleges and universities is how the Web can be used to advantage for orienting international students to the academic requirements and social opportunities of their new lives in other countries and cultures. Our purpose in this chapter is to discuss the benefits of a Web-based orientation for international students and to suggest effective means by which academic institutions can best use the Web to support their specific programs and goals with respect to international education.

Many of the complexities that arise when colleges and universities contemplate ways to orient international students come from the fact that current changes in student demographics, coupled with a fast-growing global marketplace, have meant a greater diversity of cultures and languages among the students enrolled on virtually any campus. Designing an orientation program—or even a Web site—that responds effectively to this level of diversity is difficult, and most colleges and universities do not take full advantage of all the Web has to offer in addressing these issues. This situation is unfortunate because the research literature on orienting international students clearly indicates that many international higher education students return to their countries with negative experiences of their academic life abroad (Abadi, 1999). Thus the challenge remains of how best to respond to the academic, social, personal, and financial needs of international students and how best to meet their needs as they prepare to enter into their intercultural educational experiences.

The Web and the Value of Predeparture Training

One of the great benefits of the Web is its ability to overcome spatial boundaries and thus to free orientation programs from time and space constraints. Because students do not have to be physically present at an orientation held at a particular time in a given location, orientation can begin even before the international student has left his or her home country. The value of predeparture training is crucial to the success of orienting many international students (Voss, 1999), and the Web can initiate, complement, or extend predeparture training by offering a virtual introduction to a campus and a community and to the cultural mores of a country. This aspect of Web-based orientation is also important in light of two factors: (1) the limited financial resources of an institution do not cover the cost of sending campus representatives to foreign countries to participate in predeparture training, and (2) the multiplicity of languages, cultural differences, and social structures is best addressed through a Web site that can accommodate a vast range of information and provide additional links that can respond effectively, quickly, and directly to any culture. Accomplishing these ends on a personal basis would be beyond the limits of any university's resources.

Robinson (2000) has pointed out that, although many administrators favor cultural diversity and have encouraged the recruitment and retention of an increasing number of students from different ethnic and language backgrounds, the reality is that many international students experience conflicts, especially during the transition phase when there may be a clash between old and new cultures and a struggle to reconcile them. There may be deep divisions between particular values and social conventions of the home and home country on the one hand and of school and the wider society on the other. Among the types of intercultural conflict that international students may encounter are different views of the role of women in a culture, the importance of religious observances, and the primacy of the family's interests over the rights of an individual (Ghuman, 1991). Not surprisingly, some students are neither psychologically nor emotionally prepared for life in a new culture nor for their change in social status; they are now a minority within a majority culture that is not their own. Thus there is an increasing need to find proactive measures that will increase the students' awareness of the school and community culture they will be joining. Again, if this objective is to be achieved, in part, by predeparture training, the Web can be a versatile tool for preparing students in this fashion.

The Need for Globalized Web Sites

One especially valuable aspect of Web-based orientation for international students is its high emphasis on visual imagery such as icons and interactive graphics. This capacity is important not only because of potential language barriers but also because of the differences in cognitive processing styles that exist among all learners. Smith and Woody (2000) state that multimedia presentations benefit students with high visual orientation and that students with cross-cultural language barriers tend to depend on visual cues to generate contexts and signal possible modes of interpretation. As Hayakawa (2000) indicates, a high percentage of the information presented on the Web is written in English, which non-English speakers are unable to process. Likewise, information written in other languages is unavailable to many native English speakers. Therefore, Hayakawa reasons, the best way to maximize the usefulness of the Web for international students is to design and implement visual imagery that is complemented by cross-cultural, bilingual, or multilingual instruction.

Gaine (2001) supports this approach as well, pointing out that English is the official language of approximately 8 percent of the world's population, yet the majority of on-line content for the Web is in English. Gaine argues for globalization in the development of Web sites—a process that includes being aware that users will always prefer an application that suits their own language and culture and that the best Web site will address the needs of users in many different countries. The development of this type of Web site requires addressing both technical and content issues, and the Web interface itself must be modified so that it is responsive to different cultural requirements.

Institutions seeking to use the Web globally must be willing to rethink and reengineer their Web sites and must address "the key challenges presented to usability by going global" (Gaine, 2001, p. 1). Some of the major challenges include developing a navigation scheme that goes beyond simple translation because some languages (for example, Arabic) involve a reading order that differs from English. Also, translation will often alter word lengths and phrases and result in difficulties with graphical navigation methods that may require complete screen redesign.

Translation itself is also a "minefield" (Gaine, p. 3) in that colloquialisms, slang, humor, and irony do not always translate well—or at all—to other cultures. Graphics and color present another area of complexity, especially in terms of culture-specific icons. For example, the mailbox icon, which makes sense to an American audience, may seem cryptic to people in other cultures. In this regard, testing a Web site with a target audience offers a means of addressing cross-cultural issues so that cultural sensitivity can be incorporated into any Web site.

Finally, downloads such as video streaming and other technically advanced features may not work in other parts of the world. Gaine (2001) believes that accessibility is a key factor so that a Web site is available around the clock and provides quick response times and speedy downloads of information. Nielsen (2000) recommends a simple design that will work quickly with sluggish bandwidth in other countries. Like Gaine, Nielsen advocates that the design be previewed and tested by users from the countries most likely to use the site but also discusses an icon intuitiveness test that allows international users to show the designer how well they understand the visual meaning of the icon.

Content for Web Sites

In addition to the technical issues each institution will face in establishing a Web-based orientation, there is also the question of what content will best serve the needs of international students. In the broadest terms, much of the content developed for noninternational students will also be of value to international students, who will profit from such items as the history and mission of the institution; statements of academic policies and requirements, admissions procedures, and financial aid; information on the various majors, minors, and degree programs offered; profiles of the departments and faculty; listings of on-line courses and the types of technology available to students; the calendar of events for the institution; and social events such as athletics, clubs and organizations, and picnics and other gatherings.

Beyond these items of general interest to all students, the international student will also need information on such topics as assistance with student authorization forms, work permit renewal applications, and United States visitors' visa applications. In terms of campus life, information about workshops for international students, international cultural clubs and student organizations, on-campus job opportunities, community programs, and sources of ongoing support for academic and personal concerns, including counseling programs, will help provide direction and aid. One study emphasizes the importance of training international students in computer science English so they will be able to take advantage of the information technology resources available on campus. The study emphasizes the value of the Web for introducing international students to this complex subject and helping to prepare them for the requirements of academic life (Foucou and Kubler, 1999).

An often-overlooked Web resource for international students is access to on-line dictionaries for a range of languages. One excellent link for on-line dictionaries is the Stanford [University] KSL Network Services Webster Gateway [http://www-ksl-svc.stanford.edu:5915/WEBSTER/&sid

+ANONYMOUS&user-id=ALIEN], which offers access to over seventy languages. On-line dictionaries for a home language will help the international student feel less isolated and will also aid the student in translating information received from the Web site and other sources. For institutions that cannot afford the technology to provide the Web site in multiple languages or via translation software, the option of on-line dictionaries offers another resource—albeit a limited one.

To help overcome the sense of isolation, displacement, and homesickness international students may experience, access to the newspapers of their home country is an excellent resource for reconnecting with their culture and for renewing emotional ties with the home country. The *American Journalism Review*'s "Newslink" [http://ajr.newslink.org/news.html] provides access to newspapers in Africa, Asia and the Mideast, Australia, Canada, the Caribbean, Central America, Europe, Mexico, Oceana, and South America. The Universal Currency Converter [http://www.xe.com/ucc/] provides information on the current exchange rate for the dollar in nearly a hundred countries and can be a valuable aid to international students in budgeting their money and getting a full sense of their financial options. International students applying for jobs will be aided by a fact sheet provided by the University of Virginia's University Career Services [http://www.virginia.edu/~career/?handouts/intlstud.html].

International students will also require social support in their transition to a new country, and an international student message board can be an invaluable resource as part of an orientation Web site. The message board enables international students to communicate with each other, to raise and address specific questions and concerns, to learn about the local community and what it has to offer in terms of restaurants and entertainment, and to increase a sense of community in responding to such items as English language tutoring, apartments or rooms for rent, looking for a roommate, items for sale or rent, sources of transportation, and announcements of interest to international students.

One issue that has proven highly important to international students is personal safety. Understandably, many international students feel a degree of insecurity about being in a new country in which they may be regarded as "aliens," with all the accompanying stereotypes, or in which they do not speak the language well and will not be able to seek information or help in an emergency. One research study of international students newly arrived to the United States found that safety was deemed important or very important by practically all participants. Concomitantly, many of the international students appeared unaware of available campus services such as night escorts and campus police patrols and demonstrated limited understanding of how to develop danger avoidance and coping skills (Hafernik, Vandrick, and Messerschmitt, 2001). In light of these findings, an orientation Web site for international students should not only include information on safety issues and resources but also highlight campus offices that provide safety training.

Roth (1993) has pointed out the significance of being attuned to the needs of international students with disabilities and providing appropriate resources for their guidance and aid. Roth's study focuses on providing training in sign language for deaf international students, but the study's conclusions have wide applicability, and its suggestions on making information on disability resources widely available should be incorporated into the design of an orientation Web site.

Conclusion

The guiding principle to be drawn from most of the research on orienting international students to academic life in new countries is a sensitivity to the viewpoints and feelings of the international student as a visitor to a country that is not his or her own. Certainly, these students will experience excitement, intellectual curiosity, and intrigue in such a situation, but they also will face loneliness, isolation, insecurity, and a need for emotional and social support. Thus orientations for international students need to have multiple focuses and emphases that address the special situation and complex of emotions that international students will encounter in their transition to college or graduate school.

Research studies and the practical experiences of numerous academic institutions have proven that the Web can be an exceptional tool for orienting the international student to the expectations and benefits of academic life in a new country. To the extent that colleges and universities draw on the Web as a means for ongoing orientation, the likelier will be the success of many international students. For spanning space and time and for inviting all students in all countries to participate in the academic and community life of a given institution, the Web is an institution's greatest technological ally in ensuring the academic success of every student. This aspect of the Web is perhaps most important for the international student who will need the ready and supportive context and the range of information and resources that the Web can offer—from the first predeparture orientation session through to support for the international student's job search or application to graduate schools upon graduation.

References

Abadi, J. M. "Satisfaction with Oklahoma State University Among Selected Groups of International Students." *Dissertation Abstracts International,* 1999, *60,* 08A.

Foucou, P.-V., and Kubler, N. "A Web-Based Language Learning Environment: General Architecture." *ReCALL,* 1999, *11,* 31–39.

Gaine, F. "Globalisation: The Challenges to Usability." Retrieved August 17, 2001. [http://infocentre.frontend.com/servlet/Infocentre/Infocentre?page=article&id=84]

Ghuman, P.A.S. "Best or Worst of Two Worlds? A Study of Asian Adolescents." *Educational Research,* 1991, *33*(2), 121–132.

Hafernik, J. J., Vandrick, S., and Messerschmitt, D. S. "Safety Issues for International Students in the United States." *TESL Reporter,* 2001, *33*(2), 1–9.

Hayakawa, H. "International Usability, Design Guidelines and Effectiveness of a World Wide Web-Based Instructional Program for High School Students in a Cross-Culture Learning Environment." *Dissertation Abstracts International*, 2000, *61*, 05B.

Nielsen, J. *Designing Web Usability: The Practice of Simplicity*. Indianapolis, Ind.: New Riders, 2000.

Robinson, G. D. "Administrator Views of, and Strategies for Dealing with, Conflicts Involving New Canadians." *Dissertation Abstracts International*, 2000, *61*, 06A.

Roth, H. "Teaching Sign Language to International Deaf Students." *Sign Language Studies*, 1993, *78*, 53–61.

Smith, S. M., and Woody, P. C. "Interactive Effect of Multimedia Instruction and Learning Styles." *Teaching of Psychology*, 2000, *27*(3), 220–223.

Voss, S. L. "The Cross-Cultural Adaptability Factors of Chinese and Japanese Graduate Students in Oregon's Public Universities" (Portland State University). *Dissertation Abstracts International*, 1999, *61*, 02A.

CHRISTINA MURPHY is dean of the College of Liberal Arts and professor of English at Marshall University in Huntington, West Virginia.

LORY HAWKES is senior professor of general education at DeVry University in Dallas, Texas.

JOE LAW is associate professor of English and coordinator of Writing Across the Curriculum at Wright State University in Dayton, Ohio.

6

Many Americans do not study foreign languages. And when they do, they frequently do it badly because of limitations in the American educational system. However, given a public willingness to improve the situation, there are proven models for successful foreign language teaching and learning that can be implemented in our schools.

Why Americans Don't Study Foreign Languages and What We Can Do About That

David L. Sigsbee

Growing up near an international border, in the summer I often sat on a park bench along the edge of the river that separated my country from the country across the river. On the other side, I could see homes, cars moving in traffic, and people going about their business during the day. Boats from all over the world moved up and down the river, and at our home about three miles from the water's edge, I could hear the moan of boat horns on summer nights while I was lying in bed with the windows open. And as a boy, I listened to music on the radio stations from across the river. Although I never actually went across the river until I was an adult, when I finally did, there was no problem with traveling about and dealing with the language because I had learned to speak that language at home and in school.

In a slightly different experience, one of my younger cousins came with her parents from Ohio to visit us in 1951, and my cousin was, I thought, lucky because her parents took her across the river so she could say she had been in a foreign country. However, she came back quite disappointed because, she reported, the people did not look "foreign" at all. My cousin's and my experience with this particular country, while different in reaction, is not all that surprising when you know that the other country was Canada and the river was the Detroit River, which connects the upper and lower Great Lakes and separates Canada and the United States in that part of Michigan. Not much of an international experience, you might say. But I will venture that the level of our first international experience was not untypical for an American at the time and even for many today.

NEW DIRECTIONS FOR HIGHER EDUCATION, no. 117, Spring 2002 © Wiley Periodicals, Inc.

45

Why Americans Have Problems with Foreign Languages

This brings us to a problem we have as Americans. Although we do not have an official language, we expect everyone to speak English; except for parts of the southwestern United States and some large cities, most of us can live our lives in a totally English world. And even if we leave the United States, we will find English speakers in most places because the last two successive major world powers in the world, England and the United States, spread the same language and similar cultural influences to many parts of the world. As a result, English is now so common in many places that even regional ethnic hostilities can be avoided in negotiations by having the concerned parties speak English, the neutral language, when they deal with one another. Furthermore, the study of English as a second language (ESL) continues to grow around the world, and qualified teachers of it are in high demand. Unlike English, other world languages are commonly taught as foreign languages rather than as second languages.

But as the world, including the world of education, has become global in its connections, the need to communicate with speakers of other languages at work and in social situations and to deal with them in their own cultural context has increased. In the case of business education, a student can no longer assume that the options for career choice are between domestic and international business. These two areas are now one because all business ultimately has an international connection. In other aspects of life, from leisure travel to education, you will have to deal with native speakers of many different languages, as well as with aspects of their cultures that are unlike or even conflicting with your own. But in the United States, foreign language learning and its concomitant cultural understandings have never been high on the nation's educational agenda, whereas in most European countries students have opportunities and requirements to learn a second and even a third language beginning in childhood.

Poor Language Curriculum. It is not that American students do not learn foreign languages, for a great many do, but their language study is usually not continuous. Many study foreign languages at various times in elementary, middle, and high schools and in colleges and universities; inconsistent offerings produce poor results. One reason for this is the lack of a national agenda, as mentioned earlier. Although the federal government may try to encourage foreign language study through various methods, the states themselves are responsible for the education of their citizens, and they fulfill this responsibility through local school systems. In school systems, foreign languages are not commonly considered part of the core of courses that all students must take along with other common core studies such as English, mathematics, and science. If a language is taught in the elementary schools, it is generally only for a year or two and then the study is discontinued. A language may be taken up again or for the first time in the high schools but most frequently only during the first two years of high school, which means that when students go to college it has been two years since they last studied a language. In college, many students put off foreign language studies until their junior and senior years. Thus it may have been four years for many of them since they took a language in high school. Finally, chances are that the students have changed their minds about which language to study, so there is no continuity. In such cases (and they are very common), the students graduate with little or no facility arising from long-term foreign language study. Furthermore, in times of economic stringency local school boards often look at things to take out of the curriculum, and all or parts of the foreign language programs are among the academic areas cut.

Poor Scheduling of Classes. At both the high school and college level in U.S. schools, there are scheduling hindrances. In addition to the problem of most high school students taking only two years of a foreign language and doing it in the freshman and sophomore years, there is the problem of the school year schedule. As schools experiment with block schedules, teachers in many schools report that foreign language blocks are not spaced contiguously so there is no continuous instruction over several years. As with most skill-building courses, this lack of continuity is damaging to learning. At the college level, many students do not continue to build on the skills acquired in high school; instead they switch languages and delay even that until their junior year. In addition, some colleges allow second-year courses to meet only two times a week for longer periods. This too is inimical to the process of building skills by daily practice because most students put off practice until the last minute. So if the class only meets two times a week, students only prepare two times a week. It is distressing to realize that the reason for meeting two times a week is convenience in scheduling, not pedagogical need.

To be fair to U.S. students, we must note that, in addition to programmatic deficiencies in their foreign language education, their situation differs from that of students in Europe. Students in America do not have the same opportunities or stimuli. For instance, in France students tend not to work while going to school, and they can easily be in a situation to learn from native speakers of nearby countries. There are set exams with levels of proficiency and fluency that must be reached to continue study. And teachers do not have to deal with the "client" factor and its attitude that "without your students you don't have a job" that can be found in U.S. schools.

Insufficient Numbers of Teachers. One of the real challenges in foreign language education is training primary and secondary teachers so that we have a sufficient number of teachers and they have the requisite knowledge of language and culture as well as highly developed language-teaching skills. Unfortunately, the number of foreign language majors has stayed steady at 8 percent over several decades, while the need for foreign language teachers has grown. Because of the increased demand, teachers with less-than-optimal qualifications are recruited and kept in teaching positions without a support apparatus for professional development. Furthermore, the average age of secondary foreign language teachers is increasing, and unless additional new teachers are found, there will be a sharp drop in numbers because of retirements. In this situation, it is clear that states need to aid the cadre of existing teachers, to recruit gifted undergraduates actively to become foreign language teachers, and to retain them with the prestige and rewards that such positions deserve.

Difficulties in Determining the Outcomes of Foreign Language Education. Another educational problem lies in the way we select our foreign language faculty at research universities. At such universities, which include many public and private institutions, the needs of the graduate programs are the force that drives the hiring process of foreign language faculty. The selection criteria are not based on the needs of the foreign language students and undergraduate programs but rather on the graduate school's research expectations. As a result, many faculty are hired with formally stated research expectations but with no similar requirement to meet the pedagogical needs of undergraduate students, especially those who are not majors but want to achieve fluency and proficiency in a language.

The learning outcomes of foreign language study may vary greatly because of the variety of missions in foreign language programs. We must ask what we want foreign language students to be able to do, that is, what the goal of foreign language education is. In popular agendas on foreign language outcomes, there is little agreement. It is not uncommon to hear statements from outside academia such as, "I don't want my assistant to have to learn all of that grammar. I just want her to be able to speak the language on the street" or "I want my secretary to be able to write up contracts for our company. How much training will he have to have?" The assumption in both cases is that the end can be reached quickly and cheaply. In fact, foreign language education requires small classes with many contact hours, and it is as expensive as high-quality science education. Consider the following minimum goals for foreign language study:

- To learn how to learn a language (especially applicable to the first foreign language learned)
- To expand one's sense of what it means to be human by seeing the world through the window of another language
- To learn enough to be polite in social situations
- To learn enough to be a good guest in a foreign country
- To function as an independent tourist
- To become fluent
- To become proficient

These goals, ranging from humanistic purposes to advanced practical application, can all be appropriate in a given context, and one or more might be found in any foreign language program. However, to serve the purposes of internationalizing higher education, we must look to achieving fluency (characterized by ease, naturalness, and knowledge and skill) and proficiency (characterized by a predetermined level of knowledge and skills) in communication skills.

But in our attempts to help students achieve fluency and proficiency, the level of a student's intent in learning a language must be considered. American students frequently see learning a foreign language at the college level as something they must do to earn a Bachelor of Arts or perhaps a Bachelor of Science degree. Because they have not been shown that there is a strong vocational need to study a foreign language and because the quality of their collegiate language instruction can vary a great deal, the commitment of the student and the level of intent to learn a language vary widely. And students in areas as diverse as journalism and engineering seldom take foreign language courses unless required by their curriculum to do so. We would be best served by establishing an expectation that all students will spend at least a semester abroad at a foreign educational institution or in a foreign internship. Students who do not have sufficient foreign language skills for this should have available to them in the United States applied foreign language courses for their subject area, such as are available in European countries to prepare students for work in another country.

Popular (and false) promises can also stand in the way of public understanding of how a foreign language is learned. Frequently in magazines, advertisements appear about how you can learn a foreign language at home, on your own speed, and without pain. One ad promises that you will become "fluent" in thirty days by working with a tape every day for one-half hour. And this can be done while driving your car. At the end of the time period, a student will have fluency, enabling him or her to give and receive directions, conduct casual conversation, and be culturally sensitive, among other things. Other programs will have you conducting business and reading and writing like a native speaker in 270 hours of training. Such promises are patently unrealistic, but they do create a popular aura that there is an easy way to learn a foreign language, and you can do it by yourself, should you ever need to.

Changing the Nature and Intent of Foreign Language Instruction

All that has been said so far points to some salient attitudes, circumstances, and educational shortcomings that cause American students to fall short in fluency and proficiency in foreign languages. Now we need to move to ways to remedy the situation. One thing we can do first to increase the number of American students who are proficient and fluent in foreign languages is to change the way foreign languages are taught from elementary schools through college as a matter of national policy. The aim should be continuous instruction in one foreign language for students from age six through college-level courses. Ideally, ten years of one foreign language study would be completed by the time the student enters college. In addition, it is preferable that students begin a second foreign language by the time they reach high school. There should be classes in which some subjects are dealt with completely in a foreign language, sometimes called "foreign languages across the curriculum."

A model for the standards to be applied to foreign language instruction from K–12 and beyond has been developed by a coalition of foreign language groups, which began receiving funding in 1993 to develop foreign language standards. From this beginning, part of the federal America 2000 initiative and the subsequent Goals 2000 initiative was to develop the document, *Standards for Foreign Language Learning: Preparing for the 21st Century*. This document does not set forth a curriculum or dictate course content; rather, it presents a set of standards based on the "Five C's of Foreign Language Education: Communications, Cultures, Connections, Comparisons, and Communities." Not only are standards set out but sample indicators of what is to be accomplished at each grade level are described as well. So, for example, under the first "C," Communications, Goal 1.2 is "Students understand and interpret written and spoken language on a variety of topics." Given with this goal are sample progress indicators for various grade levels. As an example, for fourth grade the progress indicator is as follows:

> Grade 4: Students comprehend the main idea of developmentally appropriate oral narratives such as personal anecdotes, familiar fairy tales, and other narratives based on familiar themes.

When applied, these standards provide consistent norms, which can be used nationally to maintain quality in foreign language education.

There are also standards to assess the fluency and proficiency of students and others who already have acquired some foreign language skills. The American Council on Teaching Foreign Languages (ACTFL) has developed the widely recognized Oral Proficiency Interview (OPI), which can be conducted in person or over the phone by a team of interviewers who compare a speaker's language functioning to a set of referenced criteria and assign a proficiency level to the skills of the person being tested. As part of quality control, testers themselves are certified and periodically recertified by ACTFL so that results are comparable from interview to interview and year to year. This system has been so effective in its validity and reliability that the American Council on Education (ACE) has made recommendations for college credit based on OPI results. Some states even use the OPI as a means of meeting teacher certification requirements in a foreign language. It is used also to validate proficiency for employment and study abroad, and for the evaluation of academic program effectiveness.

At the college level, we need to separate foreign language for communication from foreign language as a humanistic study. As it is, college and university language courses are being taught in foreign language departments, where the purpose of language education in the minds of the faculty is most often to study literature and even train literary critics. To the extent possible, we need to separate the teaching of foreign language hearing, speaking, reading, and writing skills from the humanities and the teaching of literature. It would make sense, if academic politics would allow it, to put foreign languages for communication, English composition, and oral communication courses together in one department, where all of them would be approached first as skills. This would also allow professors of literature studies, whether English, French, Chinese, or Greek, to be placed together in a literature department, where they could pursue their common educational purpose. And when colleges and universities do teach language courses for communication, they must measure students' progress at all levels by measuring their fluency and proficiency rather than the number of credit hours earned.

A proposal for educational reform such as the foregoing, which requires revamping our whole educational apparatus from kindergarten through the college baccalaureate, cannot meet the more immediate and short-term needs for college graduates who need good communication skills in a second language. However, another model does exist to meet short-term needs—the methods used at the Defense Language Institute (DLI), which provides intensive language instruction to military personnel and others for periods ranging from twenty-five to sixty-three weeks, the length depending on the language being learned. The training is tied closely to a proficiency-based curriculum, and the classes are team taught with two instructors, 90 percent of whom are native speakers. Classes are small; they meet seven hours a day, five days a week, and language work is required outside the classroom. (Students who study a language for 25 weeks spend 875 hours learning the language. In contrast, four semesters of beginning and intermediate college language study range from about 170 to 220 total hours of classroom contact in a classroom of 20 to 30.) The DLI training is effective and does produce communicators in the target language. A similar model needs to be made widely available to the civilian population.

Conclusion

There are no quick and easy solutions to the problems and deficiencies of foreign language education in the United States, all of which result in college graduates who are not proficient and fluent in a foreign language. To increase the number of college graduates who are fluent and proficient, we need to overhaul our educational priorities and practices from kindergarten through baccalaureate education. This will require a national effort. Fortunately, an excellent model to achieve this goal is already available and described in the document, *Standards for Foreign Language Learning: Preparing for the 21st Century*. At the post-secondary level, we need to reexamine our curriculum and our goals so that we achieve a seamless path in foreign language learning from kindergarten through the baccalaureate. As part of this, we may have to reorganize how the foreign language profession is constituted at the collegiate level. Finally, we need to make available to college students, postgraduates, and others intensive training of the quality and intensity that is provided by the DLI.

Note

Readers interested in the development and application of national standards and the oral proficiency interviews, as well as the history of how these were developed and the post-secondary institutions' reactions to the standards, should consult the publications and the White Papers of the American Council on the Teaching of Foreign Languages. Particularly note *National Standards in Foreign Language Education* (a collaborative project of American Council on the Teaching of Foreign Languages [ACTFL], American Association of Teachers of French [AATF], American Association of Teachers of German [AATG], American Association of Teachers of Italian [AATI], American Association of Teachers of Spanish and Portuguese [AATSP], American Classical Association/American Philosophical Association [ACL/APA], American Council of Teachers of Russian [ACTR], Chinese Language Association of Secondary-Elementary Schools/Chinese Language Teachers Association [CLASS/CLTA], & the National Council of Secondary Teachers of Japanese/Association of Teachers of Japanese [NCSTJ/ATJ]) and *The Impact on Higher Education of Standards for Foreign Language Learning: Preparing for the 21st Century* (D. James, 1998). Information can be found at the ACTFL Web site [http://www.actfl.org/], or ACTFL can be contacted directly at American Council on the Teaching of Foreign Languages, Inc., 6 Executive Plaza, Yonkers, NY 10701.

Readers interested in the European experience in second language teaching should consult the ERIC report, "Foreign Language Teaching: What the United States Can Learn From Other Countries," an extensive examination of the foreign language teaching in various countries of Europe. Information can be found at the ERIC Web site [http://www.cal.org/ericcll/countryintro.html], or ERIC can be contacted directly at ERIC Clearinghouse on Languages and Linguistics, Center for Applied Linguistics, 4646 40th Street NW, Washington, DC 20016–1859.

DAVID L. SIGSBEE is a faculty member in the Department of Foreign Languages at the University of Memphis and is interim director of academic transfer and of the General Education Program.

7

*International students, as well as American students who
study abroad, need to be aware of the lack of uniformity
when American universities evaluate a student's
credentials for admission to a university and determine
whether to transfer a student's credits from a foreign
university.*

Academic Background and Admissions to American Universities

Charles F. Abel, Arthur J. Sementelli

The three basic requirements for admission to U.S. colleges and universities
are (1) a sufficient command of the English language, (2) adequate financial resources, and (3) a strong academic record. Each college and university in the United States sets its own standards regarding English proficiency
and academic achievement. Some universities have exacting standards; others are more flexible. Consequently, whether you are admitted and the level
at which you are admitted depend on the policy of the institution you are
applying to and the equivalence between the educational system in the
United States and that in your country.

Basis for Admission

As admissions officers will be looking for equivalence between the American
student's experience and accomplishments and your experience and accomplishments within the educational system of your country, you should be
aware that the typical American student is admitted on the basis of his or
her academic performance in high school and on nationally standardized
tests. After completion of high school, students may enter either a college
or university or a two-year community college or technical school.
Community colleges and technical schools offer an array of certificates
attesting to a student's accomplishments, but none offer the bachelor's
degree, which typically requires a minimum of four years to complete at a
college or university. These certificates and the student's performance in the
community college or technical school may serve as a sufficient basis for
admission to a college or university. At the graduate level, students may
enter either a master's program (typically involving between one and three

years to complete) or a doctoral program leading to a Ph.D. after a *minimum* of three years (usually longer). Some universities require students to complete a master's degree before entering a doctoral program.

Given this pattern, as experienced by the typical American student, admissions officers typically base their decisions on your performance during the last four years of secondary school (or the equivalent in your country) and on the national secondary school examinations (or their equivalent) in your country. If you are applying to graduate school, the admissions officers look at the institution you attended that is most similar to the college or university.

Transfer of Credit

Although there is little uniformity across universities and colleges in how the grades on your transcripts are used for screening potential students, here are a few guidelines. First, courses taken abroad are unlikely to transfer unless they are a part of a specific university-approved exchange program. In all likelihood, any course credit earned from these other universities will not count toward graduation. Therefore, students must carefully consider the additional time and costs associated with transfers and negotiate any course credit prior to entry. Second, universities generally require a "B" average or better on high school (or the equivalent) transcripts, combined with the TOEFL (Teaching of English as a Foreign Language) and SAT (Scholastic Aptitude Test) exams as a basis for admission. Similarly, graduate programs often require a "B" average in undergraduate course work, combined with the TOEFL and GRE (Graduate Record Exam) or GMAT (Graduate Management Aptitude Test).

Some generalizations can also be made regarding admission requirements for students from certain broad geographic regions with a considerable history of sending students to American universities. For example, students from all Canadian provinces, save Quebec, are required to successfully complete grade 12 diploma requirements. For Quebec, the equivalent requirement is a Secondary V diploma. Further grade requirements vary with the institution to which admission is sought. Similarly, prospective students from England, West Indies, and East and West Africa must have a General Certificate of Education showing passes in a certain number of academic subjects (including English), as delineated by the particular college or university to which admission is sought. Many colleges also specify minimum acceptable scores on Caribbean Examinations Council examinations. A Hong Kong English School Certificate showing passes in a specified number of academic subjects, each with a minimum grade requirement (never lower than "C"), is typically required of students from Hong Kong, and applicants from India and Pakistan are usually required to have completed studies at a recognized institution of higher learning (that is, studies beyond the intermediate examination level with a standing specified by the university, often in the first division with a minimum grade specification).

Some universities either weight or index grade point averages from foreign countries for purposes of both undergraduate and graduate program admissions. As it is both time consuming and labor-intensive to review foreign transcripts to weight and index grades and thus transfer credits from a wide array of countries and institutions outside the United States, colleges and universities often require students to have this done for them by an independent service. How these services develop the weightings and how they apply the weights in different circumstances is unclear, as this is determined not by the universities in question but by independent firms with proprietary rights to the formulas and methods they employ. Credential evaluation firms charge a fee for this evaluation, and the fee averages around $100. For an additional fee, evaluations may be "rushed" to a college or university. In most cases, it is the role of the prospective student to purchase the service. Some of the larger services are

Academic Credentials Evaluation Institute
P.O. Box 6908
Beverly Hills, CA 90212
(310) 275–3530
(800) 234–1597
Fax: (310) 275–3528
Web site: www.acei1.com

Academic & Professional International Evaluations, Inc.
2991 Brimhall Drive
Los Alamitos, CA 90720
(562) 594–6498

American Education Research Corporation
P.O. Box 996
West Covina, CA 91793–0996
(626) 339–4404
Fax: (626) 339–9081
Web site: www.aerc-eval.com

It is important that you provide complete and accurate information and follow the directions in their packet.

Educational Credential Evaluators, Inc.
P.O. Box 514070
Milwaukee, WI 53203–3470
(414) 289–3412
Fax: (414) 289–3411
E-mail: EVAL@ece.org
Web site: www.ece.org (applications available)

Educational Records Evaluation Service
777 Campus Commons Road, Suite 200
Sacramento, CA 95825–8309
(916) 565–7475
Fax: (916) 565–7476
E-mail: EDU@eres.com
Web site: www.eres.com

International Education Research Foundation, Inc. Credentials Evaluation
Service
P.O. Box 3665
Culver City, CA 90231–3665
(310) 258–9451
Fax: (310) 342–7086
E-mail: info@ierf.org
Web site: www.ierf.org

Beyond these very general guidelines, you should be aware that some universities show a special interest in math and natural science grades (for example, calculus and chemistry grades), regardless of the course of study you intend to follow. The thinking behind this is that these courses are more or less the same all over the country, so an "A" in chemistry is probably a much more universal indicator of ability than an "A" in philosophy or art appreciation. Given the variability of admission standards, however, a less than stellar record in math and science alone is not a bar to admission in most universities. The best thing to do is to contact the institutions that interest you well in advance to determine whether there are any special conditions you may have to meet.

Conclusion

Finally, given the general unfamiliarity of most admissions officers with foreign educational practices and requirements, it may be helpful to have an official of your educational institution indicate on your transcripts what the numbers on your record mean in your academic system. For example, if you are coming from a country where only a few score in the 85th percentile, or score a 65 on a certain test, or average a 70 in grades, it is very important that you have that noted.

CHARLES F. ABEL is assistant professor of political science and director of The Knowledge Factory, a center for basic and applied research at Stephen F. Austin State University.

ARTHUR J. SEMENTELLI coordinates the undergraduate Public Administration Program at Stephen F. Austin State University.

8

To foster an appreciation of cultural similarities and differences, professors are challenged to develop professional international opportunities through faculty exchange and study abroad programs or through a host of currently existing international resources.

What Kinds of Professional International Opportunities May Be Secured for Faculty?

Samuel Fung, Joe Filippo

How do I get involved in study abroad? Do I need to know the language of a given country to teach in it? How difficult is it to adjust to the lifestyles in other countries? Can I afford to engage in research or teaching in another country? If I wish to teach a course, who would my students be? Are people in other countries conducting the same research in which I am involved? What is going on out there?

These are some of the questions and concerns that are raised among faculty members when they first consider the prospect of teaching or doing research in other countries. Such questions may arise from contact with interested international students and visiting international faculty, who, more than ever before, are coming to U.S. campuses. The resulting frequent contact with international students and faculty can motivate scholars and teachers who have not traveled abroad to do so. However, a critical step in preparing for travel abroad is for professors to question their cultural biases.

Questioning Biases

Even professors can have misconceptions about cultural differences. Professional educators occasionally generalize about cultural conditions that are basic to a given country. For example, a professor who says he would love to go to China but does not like rice suffers under the assumption that rice is an essential ingredient in every meal.

NEW DIRECTIONS FOR HIGHER EDUCATION, no. 117, Spring 2002 © Wiley Periodicals, Inc.

By their very nature, most teachers are avid readers. They tend to absorb not only facts and ideas that relate to their own culture but the seeds of other cultures are also implanted in their imaginations through the written works of others. For example, Edgar Rice Burroughs had a major impact on the thoughts of millions of early twentieth-century Americans when he introduced them to Tarzan. His efforts as an author played a large role in the development of many Americans' perceptions concerning the African continent. This monolithic approach to Africa, however, was disputed by people who had visited the great continent and knew of its many dimensions and its great variety of cultures.

International experiences enable professors to have direct interaction with the people and culture of different countries, particularly within the host country's natural setting. Such activity enriches professors' cross-cultural understanding or perspective of a country, and it may be a successful tool in the integration of our concepts and theories that govern our professional disciplines. An American who visits Asian countries such as China, for instance, will quickly discover that the Chinese rarely provide parking lots that are immediately visible to their patrons. Instead, they opt to build spaces behind the store. This stands in stark contrast with the traditional American method that places parking lots in the front of the store to attract more customers. The American soon realizes that China's different spatial arrangements speak to space availability and the aesthetic of the location.

There are many similarities and differences among cultures, and it is tempting for people to place values on each difference. Such action frequently leads to stereotyping, which can lead to both negative and positive judgments about an entire culture. International experiences can promote the idea that people should enjoy the similarities and respect the differences in other cultures.

Developing International Opportunities

To participate in international experiences, two popular ways are (1) to establish or develop one's own faculty exchange or study abroad programs and (2) to identify and enlist in currently existing programs.

Developing Faculty Exchange or Study Abroad Programs. There is a difference between faculty exchange and study abroad programs. *Faculty exchange,* as the term suggests, relies on the exchange of faculty from two or more institutions. Study abroad programs, in contrast, do not involve direct exchange of faculty from two or more institutions; they usually involve a faculty member teaching his or her own students in another country. Sometimes, however, students from other universities in the United States may be included.

A critical issue in establishing either faculty exchange or study abroad programs is to secure the support of the university administration. To facilitate this effort, it is crucial that the university include the importance of international experiences or opportunities within its mission statement. More than ever before, university mission statements and primary goals are requirements that fuel the necessary funding for international programs. Funding will be essential to encourage faculty participation.

Funding alone, however, is not enough. It is important to solicit the interest and good will of campus colleagues who have contacts with counterparts in other countries. The administration can initiate this action by sending to the faculty a survey that assesses their knowledge, experience, and interest in selected countries. With this information in hand, the administration can then determine whether it is in the university's best interest to establish a program in the faculty member's country of choice. Such an endeavor requires careful knowledge of and attention to the university's goals to ensure the success of these initial efforts.

At this point, it is necessary to analyze the geographical area and political stability of the country under consideration. The selection of the geographical area, for example, should in large part be determined by the financial considerations of the institution. This information can usually be obtained from the faculty member who seeks to coordinate the program. Additional information gleaned from government findings may be obtained through international agencies such as NAFSA (formerly "National Association of Foreign Student Advisors"): Association of International Educators (www.nafsa.org).

If an institution is financially able to develop faculty exchange and study abroad programs, several additional considerations need to be made. One of these is the type of agreement that may be made available between two institutions. Two basic types of agreement are short-term exchanges and full-term exchanges. Short-term exchanges may be for any time less than a full term; therefore, faculty will not be responsible for teaching a full course. They will instead provide special presentations from different cultural perspectives, such as lectures on the economic or cultural development of their country. Full-term exchanges may vary from one term to an academic year. In these cases, the faculty members may, for instance, have full responsibility for teaching a course or conducting a research project at the host institution. Following is an example of a faculty exchange agreement.

1. Faculty are defined as full-time employees who hold academic rank at their institution. Spouses, relatives, and alumni are not eligible for this program.
2. Faculty may attend the host institution for the purpose of research, lecture, and discussion.
3. The home institution will select and propose to the host institution the candidate and the types of activities that the candidate wishes to pursue and the resources he or she requires. The host institution will review the proposal to determine whether it has the programs and resources to accommodate the request.
4. Faculty exchanges may begin in either the summer or regular terms.

5. The period for the exchange is hereby limited to one or more terms. Aforesaid period may be extended upon mutual consent of the universities.
6. Faculty members may teach at the host institution only by mutual agreement of the two universities.
7. Exchange scholars shall receive financial assistance as determined by the host institution. The level of support will be defined in writing at the time the scholar is accepted by the host institution.
8. The host institution will provide housing and transportation back and forth from the host international airport and the host institution.
9. Participants will arrange for and pay for their own international travel and medical insurance.
10. The host institution, although under no financial obligation, will assist in making arrangements for the scholar's needs.
11. Neither institution shall be responsible for personal injury or property damage or other loss except that resulting from its own negligence or the negligence of its employees or others for whom it is legally responsible.
12. This agreement shall continue for X years but may be terminated by either institution by official, written notification duly signed by the presiding officer of the notifying party. The notice of termination must be received by the other party not later than one year in advance. Notwithstanding the termination of this agreement, it is agreed that any faculty or professional staff who have been accepted by the host university prior to the date of termination may complete their commitment as arranged under the exchange program.
13. This agreement shall be valid from the date of the signatures and may be revised, modified, or renewed by mutual agreement.

When an agreement is established between two institutions, the home institution in the United States must apply for sponsorship of an Exchange Visitor Program through the U.S. Department of State (see the end of the chapter for contact information). Once the institution has been approved as a sponsor, it will be authorized to issue IAP-66 forms to the selected faculty members to apply for J-1 "visiting scholar" visas to the United States.

Identifying Currently Existing Programs. Faculty members need not establish their own programs. Many excellent programs are available to individual faculty members who wish to participate in an international experience.

The Fulbright programs provide options to faculty and administrators. For instance, the Fulbright Scholar Program offers faculty, professionals, and teachers the opportunity to teach and to conduct research. The Fulbright Teacher and Administrator Exchange Program makes opportunities available to teachers and administrators from K–12 schools and higher education. More information can be obtained from their Web site [http://www.grad.usda.gov/info_for/ fulbright.cfm] or by e-mail at GOTOBUTTON BM_2_ fulbright@grad.usda.gov.

The Council on International Education Exchange (CIEE) sponsors an International Faculty Development Seminar series to stimulate college and university initiatives toward internationalizing curricula. The seminars provide short-term, intensive overseas experience for faculty and administrators. Seminars are designed to offer focused updates on global issues and regions that are shaping the course of world events while introducing faculty to scholarly communities overseas. The CIEE Web sites are www.ciee.org /isp and www.ciee.org/ifds. The e-mail addresses are studyinfo@ciee.org and ifds@ciee.org.

Institutions may apply for participation in various consortia throughout the United States. For example, the Cooperative Center for Study Abroad (CCSA) is a consortium of American colleges and universities with study abroad programs and internships in English-speaking regions such as Australia, Barbados, England, Ireland, Kenya, New Zealand, and Scotland. The CCSA Web site is http://www.nku.edu/~ccsa/ and the e-mail address is CCSA@NKU.EDU. Another example is the Mid-Continent Consortium for International Education. This is a newly established body that seeks to provide opportunities that are at least initially restricted to French-speaking countries. The e-mail address is paucrapo@utm.edu.

Other resources include (1) study through other institutions' study abroad programs, (2) study abroad programs sponsored by the East-West Center Program in Hawaii (see the end of the chapter for contact information), (3) the Japan Exchange and Teaching (JET) program, sponsored by the Embassy of Japan [www.embjapan.org and cgjpnola@cmq.net], and (4) *International Exchange Locator: A Resource Directory for Educational and Cultural Exchange*. This last resource is a directory of information regarding international, educational, and cultural exchange by private organizations, government agencies, and congressional committees.

Conclusion

Now more than ever it is important that the people of the world communicate successfully with one another on a personal scale. To do so demands patience, a readiness to embrace different cultures, and a passion to understand the values and motives of others. Whether professors decide to develop their own international opportunities or to pursue existing venues, the benefits derived from such efforts are well worth the risk. A good plan, well followed, can yield satisfying results that will serve both teachers and scholars and their respective institutions.

Reference

Alliance for International Educational and Cultural Exchange. *International Exchange Locator: A Resource Directory for Educational and Cultural Exchange*. Washington, D.C.: Alliance for International Educational and Cultural Exchange, 2000.

Exchange Program Addresses

Council on International Education Exchange (CIEE)
205 East 42nd Street
New York, NY 10017–5706
(212) 822–2747
Fax: (212) 822–2779

East-West Center, Program on Education and Training
1777 East-West Road
JAB 2105, Honolulu, Hawaii 96848
(808) 944–7315
Fax: (808) 944–7070

Fulbright Programs
600 Maryland Avenue, S.W.
Suite 320
Washington, DC 20024
(800) 726–0479
Fax: (202) 479–6806
E-Mail: fulbright@grad.usda.gov
Web site: www.grad.usda.gov/info_for/fulbright.cfm

Japan Exchange and Teaching (JET)
Embassy of Japan, Office of the JET Program,
2520 Massachusetts Avenue NW, Washington, DC 20008.

Mid-Continent Consortium for International Education
(MCCIE)
The University of Tennessee at Martin
Modern Foreign Languages Department
Martin, TN 38238.

U.S. Department of State, Exchange Visiting Program—ECA/GCV
State Annex 44, Room 734
301 4th Street SW
Washington, DC 20547

SAMUEL FUNG is director of international education at Austin Peay State University in Clarksville, Tennessee.

JOE FILIPPO is assistant vice president for academic affairs at Austin Peay State University.

9

This chapter explains the merits and liabilities of student exchange programs and examines the factors needed to establish successful programs.

How Valuable Are Student Exchange Programs?

Patience A. Sowa

Establishing student exchange programs is one of the ways in which U.S. and overseas institutions are working toward internationalizing higher education. In general, international education can be defined as activities and programs that encourage the flow of ideas and people across cultural and international boundaries (Arum and Van de Water, 1992; Harari, 1992). In light of this definition and for the purposes of this chapter, student exchange programs will be defined broadly as "the international movement of scholars and students" (Harari, 1992, p. 69). This would include U.S. and foreign nationals, graduate and undergraduate students, and long- and short-term programs. In addition, this definition includes the myriad of programs and activities that enable U.S. students to attend foreign universities and foreign students to attend U.S. universities.

This chapter examines the merits and liabilities of student exchange programs and discusses the factors that make for the establishment of successful programs.

Models of Student Exchange Programs

Kraft, Ballantine, and Garvey (1994) list three models of student exchange programs: total immersion, protective studies, and tour models. These researchers claim that most student exchange programs are based on either one or more of these models. The total immersion model places U.S. students in a foreign university for the duration of at least one semester but typically for a year. This model allows students to participate in academic courses and experience an in-depth study of the language and culture of the country in which they are residing. The protective studies abroad model "ties students to a U.S. program with resident advisors and instructors" and "the study tour provides an overview of a topic or countries" (p. 27). The study tour is usually short in duration, lasting from about two weeks to a summer. These models, the authors state, are neither mutually exclusive nor in conflict; the semester at sea program, for example, encompasses all three models.

Goals and Missions of Student Exchange Programs

The various goals and missions of students and institutions of higher education determine the model variety and the scope of student exchange programs. Goodwin and Nacht (1988) state that the goals of student exchange programs can range from being a grand tour to exploring one's roots to improving international relations. Kraft, Ballantine, and Garvey (1994) note that although programs in both the United States and Europe (France, Germany, Sweden, and the United Kingdom) have the goals of improved language skills and communication with foreigners, the U.S. programs also tend to focus on individual development and international understanding. Similarly, the Council on International Educational Exchange (2001) states that its goals are to promote peaceful cooperation between countries, to help individuals gain insight into their societies and those of other countries, and to enable students to learn new skills. The Fulbright/International Institute of Education (Fulbright/IIE), which offers a variety of programs for U.S. and foreign nationals, has the goal of "creating a better world community" through "investing in people" (p. 1).

Institutions of higher education and state governments also see student exchange programs as a vital way of competing in the global market place and maintaining U.S. economic strength. Fugate and Jefferson (2001) state that the academic community has fallen behind in preparing students to be "global citizens" who can compete with other nations and work and live in different countries. To prepare students for the international workforce, the Fulbright/IIE created the Work Abroad Program, which authorizes current students and recent graduates to work in countries such as Australia, Canada, Costa Rica, Great Britain, France, Ireland, and New Zealand (Meyers, 2001). In 1997, almost 5,700 American students participated in this program, which gives students the opportunity to experience total immersion through living and working in another country.

Other goals of student exchange programs are helping to improve the lives of people in developing countries through technical assistance, educational cooperation programs (Arum and Van de Water, 1992), or international service-learning. For example, students from Mennonite institutions such as Goshen College are required to spend a semester abroad in developing countries in Africa, the Caribbean, Central America, and Europe (Racette, 1996).

Merits of Student Exchange Programs

According to the research literature, the benefits of student exchange programs are many and varied. Research from the 1950s primarily focused on the effects of exchange programs with respect to students and regarding "cross-cultural interactions . . . the increase in knowledge and language skills of other countries and changes in attitudes and career goals" (Kraft, Ballantine, and Garvey, 1994, p. 29). These researchers found that students who participated in exchange programs were more reflective, more prepared to help others, more knowledgeable with respect to international affairs, and more self-confident. Nevertheless, with respect to the attitude toward the host country, researchers cited in Kraft and others state that although there was increased understanding, student attitudes were not necessarily positive. No matter the focus of study, however, the majority of research points to the fact that student exchange programs are a valuable and crucial component in internationalizing colleges and universities.

Holman (2001) divides the merits of student exchange programs into educational and organizational benefits. The former consists of personal development, increased language proficiency, and the cultivation of a "comparative perspective and cross-cultural understanding" (p. 1). The latter comprises student recruitment, alumni giving, and faculty development.

The majority of organizations and universities, however, tend to place more emphasis on the educational benefits of student exchange programs. The American Council on Education (2001) for example focuses on the improvement and development of foreign affairs. The ACE states that student exchange programs provide Americans with the experience of living in a foreign culture and foreign students with an understanding and appreciation of U.S. cultures and systems. In addition, exchange programs can be the means of developing personal relationships that can be helpful in international relations. The council states:

> The personal relationships that develop in such programs contribute to a web of interconnectedness and trust that links our country with the rest of the world. Because exchange programs involve so many people who become leaders in their own countries, they are among our most effective tools for advancing our national interests in foreign affairs. [p. 340]

The Fulbright/IIE organization, which has been successful in sustaining international exchange, also cites the merits of these programs with respect to international relations. The more than 200,000 foreign Fulbright alumni are leaders in all sectors of their countries. These alumni, the organization notes, can work to forge stronger relationships between the U.S. and their countries.

Exchange programs also help support the U.S. economy. Foreign student enrollment, for instance, has created more than 100,000 American jobs, and the nation's universities and colleges are the fifth-largest exporter of services. According to NAFSA: Association of International Educators (n.d.), during the 1999–2000 academic year, foreign students "brought almost $12.3 billion into the U.S economy" (p. 1). Furthermore, foreign students can contribute to enriching the curricula and culture of colleges and universities.

Exchange programs that send U.S. scholars and students abroad have assisted developing countries in areas such as health, the environment, and agriculture. Research in these and other areas has enabled world institutions of higher education to forge partnerships and strengthen collaborative efforts with each other (Jenkins, 1996).

Racette (1996) maintains that student exchange programs have the potential "to give students an intensive understanding of the environmental and social problems mounting in the non-industrial world as well as of their global implications" (p. 32). She also suggests that it is vital for U.S. students to have experiences in developing countries because these experiences can also lead to "developing tools of peaceful coexistence within America" (p. 32) with respect to understanding and living with immigrants. Ultimately then, international exchange programs can be beneficial to all countries involved.

Liabilities of Student Exchange Programs

The idea of international student exchange is an excellent one and can be said to have liabilities only inasmuch as students fail to participate in exchanges, programs fail, or program or student goals are not met due to factors such as the costliness of programs, the disruption of the traditional academic cycle, the length of the programs, poor institutional linkages, the lack of equal two-way exchanges with developing countries, and the poor preparation of students.

Despite increases in the number of American students studying abroad, statistics on student exchange programs indicate that, on the whole, very few American students participate in these programs. Goodman (2001) and Christie (1999) state that less than 1 percent of all Americans enrolled in higher education study abroad.

The problem of the lack of American student participation in exchange programs frequently stems from the U.S. higher education system. The literature indicates that students do not participate in these programs because they are frequently not given academic credit and feel that going abroad will lengthen their studies. Faculty members often discourage students because they feel that leaving in the junior year will "disrupt the traditional academic cycle" (Marcum, 2001, p. 1). A lack of information about and variety in programs may also lead to poor participation.

Student exchanges can be expensive in that students may have to pay for personal expenses, travel, and housing costs. Staying in cities like London or Paris can be very costly. These factors discourage students and have the consequence of attracting middle- and upper-income students and eliminating lower-income students, leading to little diversity among students who study abroad. Student exchange can also be costly for institutions of higher education in developing countries that might not have the resources to match institutions in the West. The lack of resources, as well as poor management and miscommunication, may also lead to weak institutional linkages, which can again affect the success of programs (Jenkins, 1996).

Although the numbers of students participating in exchange programs in developing countries in Africa, Asia, and Latin America have increased (American Council on Education, 2001), the majority of U.S. students still go to Europe (National Association of Foreign Student Advisors [NAFSA], 2001). Jenkins (1996) asserts that "developing countries are poorly represented in student exchange and study abroad programs" (p. 9) because areas such as sub-Saharan Africa have very few educational resources and opportunities.

Establishing Exchange Programs

To establish and maintain successful student exchange programs, universities and colleges first have to analyze their strengths and weaknesses and ascertain that they have the resources, financial and otherwise, to institute a program and sustain it for a lengthy period of time (Jenkins, 1996). In addition, presidents, administrators, faculty, and the university communities need to ensure that their goals for the programs are in line with the mission of the institution. A unity of mission and purpose among stakeholders should lead to the establishment of strong programs that are fully integrated into university curricula and life. These stakeholders, especially the administrators, have to be cognizant of the factors that have led to the success of existing programs. Essentially then, the literature indicates that to establish successful programs, universities need to focus on best practices, thereby avoiding the liabilities stated in the previous section.

Moreover, to establish successful programs, universities need to diversify and tailor student exchanges to the needs of their students. Florida State University's Beyond Borders offers short programs of a week to two weeks in Europe, the West Indies, and Latin America (Christie, 1999). Although the stay is short, total immersion is achieved through living with host families and performing community service. Christie notes that short-term programs are valuable to students who need to complete their degrees within a certain time. Moreover, these programs frequently serve as catalysts and heighten the desire of students to go abroad again for longer periods of time.

For students who do not have the means, the three-to six-month Fulbright/IIE Work Abroad Program, for example, is cost-effective in that students are employed and can pay their own expenses (Meyers, 2001).

To overcome inflexible curricular requirements, and to encourage the participation of nontraditional students and students in underrepresented areas such as the sciences and engineering, Marcum (2001) recommends that colleges and universities offer these students the opportunity to participate in short-term programming. For example, they could go abroad over two summers or for two weeks. Other alternatives he suggests are developing pre-major study abroad programs, or on-line courses.

The development of on-line courses, as well as strong institutional linkages with the curricula of overseas institutions, should address the concern of many faculty members that student exchange programs are frequently not academically rigorous (Kraft, Ballantine, and Garvey, 1994). Wherever these programs are considered to be academically rigorous, students should be given academic credit.

Establishing strong and sustainable linkages with institutions abroad is also vital in instituting successful student exchange programs. Linkages between institutions can be made strong through effective program design, which, as Jenkins (1996) asserts, provides a "way to set priorities, encourage open communication, and establish a working environment that recognizes the impact of organizational history and organizational culture" (p. 13). In the case of developing countries, both sides also need to understand and work to avoid the political and economic issues, as well as institutional resources that might cause problems and prevent the maintenance of successful programs (Jenkins, 1996).

Program designs should also include thorough orientation programs for both U.S. and foreign students. These programs can help students understand and deal with culture shock and prepare them for living and working in a different culture.

Collaboration through statewide, regional, federal, or international consortia can also help establish successful student exchange programs (Jenkins 1996; Pickert, 1992). Using consortia, Pickert (1992) notes, leads to the sharing of manpower, administrative resources, and costs. In addition, participation in such groups helps to further internationalize the curricula of participating institutions. According to Pickert, "consortia seem highly successful in helping institutions with limited resources widen opportunities in international education" (p. 53).

Finally, programs should institute different forms of assessment, which can help students, communities, faculty, and administrators examine the study abroad experience. By doing so, stakeholders can determine whether their goals have been achieved.

Conclusion

The concept of student exchange goes far back in human history. Scholars, students, and institutions of higher education then and now realize the importance of forging links for learning, developing personally, global understanding, and peacemaking. Currently, people have also realized how interdependent nations have become and therefore how crucial it is to encourage and foster the internationalization of higher education through student exchange programs. As this chapter indicates, the value of these programs far outweighs any liabilities they might have.

References

American Council on Education. "Educating for Global Competence." In P. O'Meara, H. D. Mehlinger, and R. M. Newman, (eds.), *Changing Perspectives on International Education.* Bloomington, Ind.: Indiana University Press, 2001.

Arum, S., and Van de Water, J. "The Need for a Definition of International Education in U.S. Universities." In C. B. Klasek, B. J. Garavalia, and K. J. Kellerman (eds.), *Bridges to the Future: Strategies for Internationalizing Higher Education.* Carbondale, Ill.: Southern Illinois University at Carbondale, 1992.

Christie, R. (ed.). *Beyond Borders: A Model for Student and Staff Development.* New Directions for Student Services, no. 86. San Francisco: Jossey-Bass, 1999.

Council on International Educational Exchange. Principles of good practice for international education. Retrieved September 1, 2001, from http://www.ciee.org

Fugate, D. L., and Jefferson, R. W. "Preparing for Globalization: Do We Need Structural Change for Our Academic Programs?" *Journal of Education for Business,* 2001, *76,* 160–166.

Fulbright/IIE. Available from www.iie.org/fulbright/

Goodman, A. E. "Education in a Global Age." Speech before the annual convention of the American Association of State Colleges and Universities. Retrieved September 3, 2001 from http://www.iie.org

Goodwin, C., and Nacht, M. *Abroad and Beyond: Patterns in American Overseas Education.* Cambridge: Cambridge University Press, 1988.

Harari, M. "The Internationalization of Curriculum." In C. B. Klasek, B. J. Garavalia, and K. J. Kellerman (eds.), *Bridges to the Future: Strategies for Internationalizing Higher Education.* Carbondale, Ill.: Southern Illinois University at Carbondale, 1992.

Holman, M. A. "Cooperation and Collaboration in U.S. Study Abroad Programming." Open Doors on the Web, Council for International Educational Exchange. Retrieved September 4, 2001 from http://www.opendoorsweb.org

International Institute of Education. "IIE's Mission." Retrieved September 2, 2001 from http://www.iie.org

Jenkins, K. "Designing Sustainable Educational Linkages with Institutions in Developing Countries." *International Review,* 1996, *6,* 9–29.

Kraft, R. J., Ballantine, J., and Garvey, D. "Study Abroad or International Travel: The Case of Semester at Sea." *International Review,* 1994, *4,* 23–61.

Marcum, J. A. "What Direction for Study Abroad? Eliminate the Roadblocks." *Chronicle of Higher Education,* May 18. Retrieved September 3, 2001 from http://www.chronicle.com

Meyers, J. "Models for the Future: Linking Academic and Experiential Programs in Education Abroad." Open Doors on the Web, Council on International Education. Retrieved September 4, 2001 from http://www.opendoorsweb.org

NAFSA: Association of International Educators (n.d.). "Data on International Education." Retrieved November 13, 2001 from http://www.nafsa.org/content /PublicPolicy/DataonInternationalEducation/FactSheet.htm

Pickert, S. "Achieving an International Perspective in Higher Education." Report 2, ASHE-ERIC Higher Education Reports. Washington D.C.: George Washington University, 1992.

Racette, D. "Study Abroad in the Non-industrial World: Problems and Potentials." *International Review,* 1996, *6,* 31–41.

PATIENCE A. SOWA is assistant professor of education at Rockhurst University in Kansas City, Missouri. Her areas of interest are TESOL and literacy teaching and learning.

10

When professors bring their families with them to a new country, adjustment concerns are magnified. This chapter outlines the challenges families will face and suggests preventative tips and resources for helping them cope.

Family Adjustment to American Culture

Carolyn Davidson Abel

A certain culture shock occurs when anyone enters an unfamiliar setting and cannot navigate easily among the expectations, attitudes, values, and assumptions already in place (Berry, 1990; Furnham and Bochner, 1986; Liebkind, 1996; Weaver, 1993). When family members come along, adjustment problems multiply (Chi-Ching, 1995; Liebkind, 1996; Reynolds and Bennett, 1991). Although family stress is presumably inevitable with any stay beyond the short term (Furnham and Bochner, 1986), we are now discovering that personal expectation and previous experience can interact with certain conditions encountered in the new setting to predispose family members to more or less of this acculturative stress (Berry and Annis, 1974; Furnham and Bochner, 1986; Hall and Whyte, 1960; Liebkind, 1996; Miranda and Umhoefer, 1998). Although unable to provide solutions tailored to meet specific individual needs, this chapter describes some general stages family members can expect to encounter and offers strategies and resources for helping them adjust.

Stages of Adjustment

Brink and Saunders (1976) outline four stages of culture shock. Although family members will likely pass through these stages at different times, further complicating matters (Liebkind, 1996), awareness of these stages can help offset some of the negative impact (Matheny and others, 1986; Winkelman, 1994). The first is called the honeymoon phase. In this stage, new arrivals typically look forward to their new experience with positive anticipation.

Within half a year, the second stage—disenchantment—erupts. Feelings of isolation and loneliness surface. Newcomers have difficulty penetrating the veneer of their new world and become frustrated, even angry. They miss family and friends. Stress mounts and culture shock sets in.

The third stage is called beginning resolution. As family members reluctantly rise to meet the challenge, they make friends and become noticeably confident as they gain in their ability to navigate the new system. Some of those initial negative reactions are now replaced with an ironic sense of humor. In fact, humor and a positive outlook can have far-reaching effects on one's ability to adjust to any new situation (Anderson, 1994).

The final stage probably has something to do with the reliable old adage, "life is like a mirror." In this phase, called effective function, family members become remarkably comfortable and fully integrated. In fact, were they to return home, reverse cultural shock would occur. Their lives are finally in control, and a bit of wisdom has been gained for all the effort (Anderson, 1994). Success begets success; life is good.

Bennett (1986) discusses six levels of adjustment. These are similar to those of Brink and Saunders in transitioning from frustration through accommodation to assimilation, but Bennett focuses on achieving cultural sensitivity from an initial perception of loss. His first stage is denial. Family members are highly resistant to the new culture and find absolutely no value in it. During the second stage—the defensive stage—they begin acknowledging their new surroundings but still consider their own culture superior. Stage three sees some merging of the two cultures; stage four finds respect for both, and stage five results in being adept at switching from one to the other. In stage six, an ability to move comfortably between both is reached.

Understanding and anticipating these stages can help ameliorate many of them. When aware of what is happening, family members are more in control over how they perceive and might handle their lives (Winkelman, 1994).

Coping Resources

Berry (1990) and Matheny and others (1986) state that no matter what problems newcomers may face, much of the stress is triggered by the lack (or perceived lack) of adequate resources for solving them. Empirical research supports the critical role these coping resources play in preventing excessively negative reactions to acculturative stress (Fleishman, 1984; Hobfoll, 1989). The rest of this chapter is devoted to providing an arsenal of tips and guidelines intended to help families tackle the frustrations involved in moving to and living in America.

Your Family Comes First

Once you arrive, your children will need your primary attention. If you can manage to get them settled and comfortable, more time will be available for you. When children protest the move from the outset, this process must begin earlier. Involve them in the planning. This helps them gradually acclimatize to the idea, as they begin focusing on the more salient aspects of the move. You may want to purchase an audiotape player with earphones or a portable electronic game for that long trip across the ocean and the many hours you will spend searching for your new home. Include them when you can, as you decide which home will be most suitable for your family. Consider proximity to playgrounds and schools when choosing a location.

Once you move into your new home, spend time making your children's bedrooms special and comfortable. Remind them that their friends and family are only an e-mail, phone call, or letter away. Create a small writing kit, complete with colorful postcards, stamps, and all of their old friends' addresses and phone numbers. Be sure to distribute your new home address and phone number to old friends and family as soon as possible. Children will maintain these ties until they are comfortable enough to replace them with new interests.

Take time with your children to explore your new community. Show them what they can do there. A trip to the local playground, a family picnic in the park, even a ride around the block to see where biking and meeting new friends might be established, all help your children gain a sense of greater security and comfort in their new surroundings.

Other professors in your university department can be a great resource for additional ideas and direction. Encourage them to join you with their families after work for fast food, ice cream, or trips to the movies together. Build these ties early (Furnham and Bochner, 1986; Liebkind, 1996; Vogel, 1986). You might also ask them who is sponsoring exchange students from other countries; try to get these children together with yours before the first day of school.

Shop once a week with your children and together select a new food to take home and prepare. Have fun with your reactions to these new tastes and experiences. Help your family understand how the two cultures differ and that both have exciting value. For some, this may be the first time they discover that they even have a culture (Hall and Whyte, 1960). The following Web site can help you find and joke about the many, sometimes funny, differences between cultures: http://www.edupass.org/culture/.

Hang tight to the old while acclimating slowly to the new. You're all in this together. Establishing routines and special times as a family unit will be very important now. Have dinner at the same time each day and find time for reading books just before bedtime. Take a moment to notice how life has changed for each family member. Wives especially may be feeling some tension with the significant role change they may be enduring (Vogel, 1986).

Join the local library and visit as a family. The staff will be helpful in recommending resources to you. Most libraries have a film-lending service that can help your family get to know even more about life in America. Select from the generous options in the family section, and plan to watch a video together each week with an all-American favorite—popcorn. These special times together will have huge payoffs.

Model for your family how you handle the ups and downs of living in a new place, attendant with all of the frustrations that are natural with any change. From time to time, try to inject a little humor. Nothing lasts forever. This too shall pass.

Education: Public Schools

Children between the ages of five and eighteen are required to attend school in America. To enroll your child in school, visit the local school with your child and complete the required registration forms. Bring all important papers with you, such as Social Security cards, birth certificates, new and old addresses, home and work phone numbers, immunization records, and past school records. Ask if you may make a photocopy of the more extensive forms you complete; you can refer to them when filling in the many similar forms requested of you throughout the school year. If your child has special needs, make this known during your initial school visit. Ask about any special programs your school may offer (for example, remedial, gifted, music, art, sports, and after-school programs).

Once school registration is completed, take your child on a tour of the school. If you have young children, stop in to meet the teacher. The best time is usually a few minutes following dismissal when the teacher can give you her undivided attention. This will give both teacher and student a clearer picture of what to expect on that very important first day. You might also ask the principal if you can sit in on a class taught by your child's teacher. If you find a comfortable fit, great; if not, consider a local private school or even home schooling. Schools and teachers vary quite a bit from grade level to grade level and from school to school. Taking time now to make the best choices can save you some unnecessary aggravation and tears later. Even a decision as simple as whether to send your child to school on the free school bus should not be taken lightly. Children who ride these buses are generally unsupervised and may tease or influence your child negatively. Over time, this can have a costly impact.

If you have an older child, pay close attention to the courses he or she selects upon entering middle school and high school. If you do not understand, politely and persistently ask until you do. With so many students to keep track of, counselors cannot always give every child that special attention he or she may need. Parents must play advocate for their own children. Because peers become a dominant element in young adolescent lives (Price and others, 1985), inviting your children's friends to your home allows you to participate at least indirectly in your child's selection of friends and activities.

Encourage your child to join the band, swim team, or some other sport or after-school function. This will keep him or her healthy and constructively engaged during those normally stressful and independent adolescent years. Anything you can do to support your teen through this extra-sensitive period without unduly controlling him or her will be time worth investing.

Following are Web sites that will provide you with additional information about schooling options:

Public Schools: http://nces.ed.gov/ccd/pubschuniv.html
Private Schools: http://nces.ed.gov/surveys/pss/locator/
Blue Ribbon Schools: http://www.ed.gov/offices/OERI/BlueRibbonSchools
    /index.html
Home Schooling: http://www.eric.ed.gov/archives/homesch.html
State Regulation of Private Schooling: http://www.ed.gov/pubs/RegPrivSchl/
Accredited Early Childhood Programs: http://www.naeyc.org/accreditation
    /center_search.asp

Value of Support Groups

The "welcome wagon" is a pleasant surprise for newcomers, and most communities have them. A welcome wagon is made up of local volunteers who give their time toward making new members in the community feel welcome. They hold get-togethers and give out welcome baskets full of coupons and discounts at local restaurants and shopping malls. They can also refer you to competent doctors, dentists, plumbers, electricians, churches, and reputable private schools and day care facilities in the area.

Your college exchange program will also be a valuable resource. Such programs offer special orientations, support groups, and even bus tours both locally and throughout the United States. You should take advantage of these (Vogel, 1986); they give your family a much-needed opportunity to meet others who are sharing a similar experience while teaching you more about your new community.

Consequences of Freedom

In the United States, individuals from many backgrounds, beliefs, and persuasions find support and connection by joining one or more of the many cultural, religious, and support groups available throughout the country. Although many are "just the thing" for someone new to the United States, some can be shady or outright dangerous, preying upon unsuspecting juveniles and newcomers. Your welcome wagon group and your university will be able to steer you toward reputable clubs and groups in your area. You should remain cautious when advertisements appear unsolicited in your mail, by phone, at your door, or on TV, and you should not open your door or give out personal information to anyone you do not know. It is also a good idea to restrict much of your activity to the daylight and early evening hours and stay in the safer areas in your community until you get to know the area better.

Large cities are fraught with more crime and are simply more difficult to navigate than smaller cities. Tiny towns, however, may be so small that most community members will either be related by blood to each other or so similar that it will be difficult for you not to be conspicuous. Although some in these smaller communities will be eager to meet you, many may show some prejudice and be negative, often more out of ignorance and fear of the unknown than for any other reason. College towns are the most suitable environments for the international visitor, as members in these communities are usually more educated and eager to partake in the exciting international flavor a variety of cultures offers them. When you heed these simple tips, your life here can be a safe and pleasant one.

Jobs for Spouses

Women should not be misled into thinking that it is either necessary or desirable for all women in America to be employed. What is new in America is that whether a woman works is finally an option. Getting a job in the United States may take some time and patience. Be friendly and organized and try to convince employers that what you have done in the past can support you in the position you are seeking. Some interesting jobs you might consider include teaching English or another language, conducting informational tours at museums, and making presentations for companies involved in international exchanges for their employees. Don't forget to contact your new friends and acquaintances for their suggestions.

A Final Word

Studies reveal the primary key to achieving participation and satisfaction in America is education; the more educated you are, the easier it will be. Lazarus, Kanner, and Folkman (1980), Mezirow (1991), and Anderson (1994) have begun investigating this in depth, making a rather compelling argument for comparing level of education to one's ability to adapt to any change in life. These research results should be encouraging news for faculty members and their families who tend to be well educated. With this added edge and the resources and suggestions offered herein, faculty exchange families should find ample tools to support them through a successful pioneering adventure into their exciting new global frontier.

References

Anderson, L. "A New Look at an Old Construct: Cross-Cultural Adaptation." *International Journal of Intercultural Relations,* 1994, *18*(3), 293–328.
Bennett, M. "A Developmental Approach to Training for Intercultural Sensitivity." *International Journal of Intercultural Relations,* 1986, *10*(2), 179–196.
Berry, J. W. "Psychology of Acculturation." In R. W. Brislin (ed.), *Applied Cross-Cultural Psychology.* Newbury Park, Calif.: Sage, 1990.
Berry, J. W., and Annis, R. C. "Acculturative Stress: The Role of Ecology, Culture, and Differentiation." *Journal of Cross-Cultural Psychology,* 1974, *5*(4), 382–406.

Brink, P. J., and Saunders, J. M. "Cultural Shock: Theoretical and Applied. In P. Brink (ed.), *Transcultural Nursing: A Book of Readings*. Englewood Cliffs, N.J.: Prentice Hall, 1976.

Chi-Ching, Y. "The Effects of Career Salience and Life-Cycle Variables on Perceptions of Work-Family Interfaces." *Human Relations*, 1995, *48*(3), 265–284.

Fleishman, J. A. "Personality Characteristics and Coping Patterns." *Journal of Health and Social Behavior*, 1984, *25*, 229–244.

Furnham, A., and Bochner, S. *Culture Shock: Psychological Reactions to Unfamiliar Environments*. London: Methuen, 1986.

Hall, E., and Whyte, W. "Intercultural Communication: A Guide to Men of Action." In P. Brink (ed.), *Transcultural Nursing: A Book of Readings*. Englewood Cliffs, N.J.: Prentice Hall, 1960.

Hobfoll, S. E. "Conservation of Resources: A New Attempt at Conceptualizing Stress." *American Psychologist*, 1989, *44*, 513–524.

Lazarus, R. S., Kanner, A. D., and Folkman, S. "Emotions: A Cognitive-Phenomenological Analysis." In R. Plutchik and H. Kellerman (eds.), *Emotion: Theory, Research, and Experience*. New York: Academic Press, 1980.

Liebkind, K. "Acculturation and Stress: Vietnamese Refugees in Finland." *Journal of Cross-Cultural Psychology*, 1996, *27*(2), 161–180.

Matheny, K. B., Aycock, D. W., Pugh, J. L., Curlette, W. L., and Canella, K. A. "Stress Coping: A Qualitative and Quantitative Synthesis with Implications for Treatment." *The Counseling Psychologist*, 1986, *14*, 499–549.

Mezirow, J. *Transformative Dimensions of Adult Learning*. San Francisco: Jossey-Bass, 1991.

Miranda, A. O., and Umhoefer, D. L. "Depression and Social Interest Differences Between Latinos in Dissimilar Acculturation Stages." *Journal of Mental Health Counseling*, 1998, *20*, 159–171.

Price, J. H., Jurs, S. G., Jurs, J., Rhonehouse, M., and Isham, K. "An Empirical Test of Cognitive Social Learning Model for Stress Moderation with Junior High School Students." *Journal of School Health*, 1985, *55*(6), 217–220.

Reynolds, C., and Bennett, R. "The Career Couple Challenge." *Personnel Journal* (Mar. 1991), 46–48.

Vogel, S. H. "Toward Understanding the Adjustment Problems of Foreign Families in the College Community: The Case of Japanese Wives at the Harvard University Health Services." *Journal of American College Health*, 1986, *34*(6), 274–279.

Weaver, G. R. "Understanding and Coping with Cross-Cultural Adjustment Stress." In R. M. Paige (ed.), *Education for the Intercultural Experience*. Yarmouth, Me.: Intercultural Press, 1993.

Winkelman, M. "Cultural Shock and Adaptation." *Journal of Counseling and Development*, 1994, *73*(2), 121–126.

CAROLYN DAVIDSON ABEL *is an assistant professor in the Department of Elementary Education at Stephen F. Austin State University in Nacogdoches, Texas.*

11

When members of the campus community decide either to initiate or to expand existing opportunities for study abroad, they will need a road map for internationalizing the campus.

Internationalizing the Campus: What Do You Need to Know?

Beth H. Carmical

So your campus has decided to internationalize. Whether this decision is a new frontier for your university or an expansion of current offerings, internationalizing your campus is an exciting endeavor. But it can be quite complex. Small campuses may feel particularly intimidated when they look to larger campuses for ideas, models, and resources. Campuses with ten thousand or more students often have entirely separate divisions with specialists in international admissions, travel arrangements, immigration, study abroad, risk management, international student life, and faculty exchange. How can these things be managed on a small campus without an army of experts? How can you keep current on issues of health insurance, liability, and personal safety and relay the necessary information to your travelers and international residents? What do you need to know to embark on a successful program?

Don't Try to Internationalize Alone

If you haven't already, join a professional association at the national or state level whose mission is to further international education. Members of these organizations have realized the pitfalls of solo attempts to internationalize a campus and have elevated the practice of information sharing to the extent that workshops and roundtables can be reminiscent of pot-luck dinners where everyone brings something to share. The "cooks" offer samples of letters, forms, releases, applications, and procedures that are almost always shared with an urging to "adopt this form to your needs." Photocopies are more often than not offered with an open admission that the source of a document was a colleague who first shared the form. This propensity to cir-culate information within a professional organization, combined with access to listservs and electronic subscription services, allows access to the exper-tise of hundreds if not thousands of international education professionals. This expertise can be very quickly tapped regarding current issues and events.

One such organization is the NAFSA: Association of International Educators. For newcomers in the study abroad and foreign student advis-ing arenas, NAFSA offers basic reference materials that should be a part of your library. Foremost among them are *NAFSA's Adviser's Manual of Federal Regulations Affecting Foreign Students and Scholars* and *NAFSA's Guide to Education Abroad for Advisers and Administrators*. NAFSA also offers a Professional Development Program with a series of workshops that will help bring a novice up to par on international education issues; as an added ben-efit, workshop instructors and participants may expand your network of contacts. The NAFSA Web site is http://www.nafsa.org.

You also need to work with various groups on your campus to support your internationalizing efforts. What is the quality of your relationship with key campus constituents? Is the administration supportive? Have you estab-lished a positive working relationship with your campus controller, student health division, student affairs office, housing department, the registrar, uni-versity provost, attorney, deans, financial aid office, department chairs, and faculty? You will need cooperation from all these areas and more to succeed. Faculty members are particularly critical to the vitality of exchange pro-grams, for they often refer ideal exchange candidates to you and provide let-ters of recommendation. Also where staff is limited, budgets tend to be limited. Your faculty can serve as your connection to the world beyond. Of all categories of campus employees, faculty members are among the most likely to travel or study abroad, and they can be a valuable resource to you and your program.

A Road Map for Developing Study Abroad Programs

Suppose you have a newly established faculty-student exchange program in a foreign country, and a candidate who is very likely to qualify has come to you for assistance. Now what? What follows is a skeletal checklist—a roadmap for navigating through the complexities of study abroad programs. Keep in mind, though, that your own checklist will vary due to individual campus regulations, state law, host country law, or changes in federal law.

(I'd like to add a caveat here. In the aftermath of the September 11, 2001 tragedies, there has been a flurry of changes and proposed changes in immigration and security legislation. Regulations regarding domestic secu-rity and the safety of Americans abroad will no doubt be subject to sweep-ing changes. In light of this rapidly changing field and the need to be abreast of the latest advisories, it is more important than ever that international educators avail themselves of an efficient and reliable means of monitoring the current status of these issues.)

Remember that the time needed to travel the road map may take several months to complete. Set your deadlines accordingly. Here, then, is what you will need for your trip.

First, you'll need to make an application. Before you do, review application forms from campuses of similar size and also from campuses with respected, established programs. A handy reference when developing your own application packet is *Forms of Travel: Essential Documents, Letters, and Flyers for Study Abroad Advisers*. This is a collection of documents used by study abroad contributors from around the country who have given permission for these forms to be used, duplicated, or incorporated to suit the needs of other advisers.

After you have drafted an application, have your legal counsel review the application and supporting forms. Your attorney may also make a recommendation regarding the age at which a student may apply for certain programs without the signature of a parent or guardian. After all, your program guidelines need not be limited by what is considered to be legal age under federal or state law.

After you have reviewed several application packages, you will discover that many common elements emerge:

- *Study plan (student).* The study plan for first choice and alternate programs of study must be approved. Every effort should be made to meet the student's academic course needs during the foreign study experience so that the semester's work will keep the student on track for graduation. Prior approval by advisers, department chairs or deans, and the registrar will greatly facilitate the awarding of credits upon completion. Determine whose approval you will need on your campus and what documentation they will require.
- *Teaching plan (faculty).* Presumably this requirement would have already been met through a grant-sponsoring organization or the host institution.
- *Recommendations.* An international education adviser cannot be personally familiar with every applicant. Guidelines for recommendation letters and forms should solicit input on maturity level, emotional stability, adaptability, personal integrity, and scholastic ability. You may wish to include a faculty and a nonfaculty recommendation.
- *Academic transcript.* Obtain official, sealed documentation of the student's postsecondary academic progress. A student's scholastic performance (for example, grade point average) should meet campus requirements for study abroad.
- *Foreign language proficiency.* Your student (or faculty member) must meet foreign language requirements as established by your campus, the host institution, or the agency sponsoring the exchange programs.

- *Special needs survey.* The home and host campuses need to be equally informed about an applicant's medical and psychological history, as well as any special physical or educational needs that may be intensified under the stress of studying in a foreign country. (Such a disclosure should be used as a basis for providing assistance, not as a reason for exclusion from a program.)
- *Essay.* For faculty, this is likely to be a requirement of a grant-sponsoring institution. For students, institutions often require essays on topics such as "Why I Want to Study Abroad" or "Why I Want to Study in (name of country)." Other approaches such as requiring an essay on "Anticipated Cultural and Educational Differences in (name of country)" help prepare students for the culture shock they will no doubt experience soon after arrival.
- *Application fee.* As approved by your institution or as may be required by an external agency.
- *Budget.* This worksheet should balance anticipated costs with known sources of revenues.
- *Contact information and permission.* Obtain permission to communicate with a parent or guardian (or other primary designee) regarding all study abroad issues (including health, personal conduct, academic performance, and student account information). You will need freedom to contact this person before, during, and after the study abroad experience.
- *Student conduct contract.* A student should submit to the terms of a code of conduct that cast a wider net than the code that may appear in your campus student handbook, including such concerns as respect for local tradition, respect for property, alcohol and illegal drug use, responsibilities as a campus ambassador, and notification of whereabouts (for example, contact information during a weekend excursion and approximate return time).
- *Additional forms.* Additional forms may be required by the host institution or a coordinating agency.
- *Consent for release of student records.* Judicial proceedings (in accordance with FERPA [Family Educational Rights and Privacy Act]) should be included.
- *Financial aid.* You may wish to refer a student to a financial aid counselor. Financial aid money (grants, loans, or scholarships) is generally applicable to study abroad.
- *Passports and visas.* Passports, visas, and related documentation may take weeks or even months to obtain. Students and faculty should apply for these as soon as they are tentatively approved to participate in an exchange program.
- *Health insurance coverage.* Obtain such coverage as may be required by your campus, the host country, or host institution. If no standard is set, seek advice from a reputable, long-established firm that specializes in health insurance for students and scholars traveling abroad.

- *Predeparture orientation.* A comprehensive orientation program for out-bound students should be required by the home campus as a prerequisite to study abroad. In the "Practical Details" section of the "Pre-departure Orientation and Reentry Programming" chapter of *NAFSA's Guide to Education Abroad for Advisers and Administrators,* Hoffa and Pearson (1997) offer a checklist of orientation items.
- *Handbook.* A handbook covering issues related to study abroad will be invaluable to the student and a timesaver to you in the long run, providing students with information they need before or after the orientation session. The handbook will serve to reinforce information shared at the orientation. The orientation session and handbook should complement, not mirror, one another.

Other Sources

Obviously, all the information a student or exchange adviser might need cannot be covered here. What follows are sources you will want to add to your student and adviser toolkits for traveler preparedness.

The U.S. Department of State Web site provides a wealth of information on such topics as

Background Notes (country-specific information)
Bureau of Public Affairs
http://www.state.gov/r/pa/bgn/

Passport Services and Information
http://travel.state.gov/passport_services.html

Information on Travel Safety Abroad in Light of the Current World Situation
The Bureau of Consular Affairs
http://travel.state.gov/

Travel Warnings/Consular Info Sheets
http://travel.state.gov/travel_warnings.html

Travel Publications
http://travel.state.gov/travel_pubs.html

Some of the linked topics at this site include

Crisis Abroad
Travel Warning on Drugs Abroad
A Safe Trip Abroad
Tips for Students

Foreign Entry Requirements (for U.S. citizens traveling abroad)
Medical Information for Americans Traveling Abroad
U.S. Consuls Help Americans Abroad

Foreign Embassies in Washington, D.C.
http://www.embassy.org/embassies/index.html

CDC Summary of Health Information for International Travel
The Blue Sheet
http://www.cdc.gov/travel/blusheet.htm

Vaccination and Health Information for Travelers to Regional Destination
Links at CDC National Center for Infectious Diseases: Traveler's Health
   Destinations
http://www.cdc.gov/travel/destinat.htm

Travelers Health
Safe Food and Water
http://www.cdc.gov/travel/foodwater.htm

Foreign Entry Requirements
U.S. Department of State
Bureau of Consular Affairs
http://travel.state.gov/foreignentryreqs.html

Departure Checklists

Once your candidate for a study abroad program is processed and preparing to leave, you should provide him or her with the following frequently offered tips:

- Pay campus fees (tuition and housing) as may be required under terms of the exchange agreement.
- Terminate existing contracts with student housing and dining services.
- Arrange for campus post office to forward mail.
- Make flight arrangements.
- Appoint a power of attorney to conduct stateside transactions on your behalf.
- Collect all visa- and entry-required documentation, including health and immunization records.
- Take recommended amount of money with you, not an excessive amount. See if your U.S. bank can arrange for you to obtain $100 to $200 in the currency of the destination country so that you will have means to negotiate immediately on arrival.

- Pack credit cards, debit cards, or phone cards. Determine whether your cards can be used in the host country.
- Purchase rail passes, hotel cards, and international student I.D. cards as needed.
- Talk with your family about emergency situations and procedures to cope with them.
- Pack all medications and prescriptions (in original containers). Be sure to include extra glasses, contact lenses, and solutions.
- Check with your adviser to make sure that you are registered or otherwise "bookmarked" in campus databases during your semester abroad.

A Road Map for Incoming Non-Native Students and Faculty

Although it was possible to attempt a bare-bones checklist for outbound study abroad or exchange programs, it is impossible to reduce the immigration of students and faculty to any type of abbreviated reference that would fit within the covers of this journal. For this complex subject, it is necessary to offer a very basic introduction and provide you with leads to additional information. This chapter will be most helpful to campuses or individuals who are new to immigration.

Searching the ocean of immigration regulations for a single bit of information or in a quest for basic comprehension is overwhelming, but reviewing the regulations is a must. (See "Laws, Regulations and Guides of the Immigration and Naturalization Service" [INS] at http://www.ins.usdoj.gov /graphics/lawregs/index.htm.) Even the revered *NAFSA Adviser's Manual* is intimidating to newcomers, as it contains several pounds of loose-leaf pages.

An excellent source for building a logical frame of reference to immigration regulations is the homepage of the Office of the General Counsel of the Catholic University of America (CUA) [http://counsel.cua.edu]. Prepared for internal use by the university and its agents, the Office of the General Counsel has demystified much of the process, succinctly explaining sources of authority, how an institution qualifies, who is responsible, and the nature of specific responsibilities. The CUA internal memoranda are not intended to be viewed as a legal treatise on immigration. The great benefit to be derived from the efforts of the CUA General Counsel is that they are presented in such a manner that a reader can understand in very basic terms the different visa classifications and how they are administered. (For specific information about visas, see Chapter Four.)

A convenient form of quick reference on immigration and employment regulations, as they relate to many types of visas, is a wall chart entitled *Immigration Classifications and Legal Employment of Foreign Nationals in the States* (Rawson, 2001). This is a straightforward poster that you will want to display in your office. To make your job easier, you might consider providing copies to your colleagues in financial aid, the controller's and human resources offices, and your local Social Security Administration.

Conclusion

International education is a complicated affair, so if you are inexperienced and beginning to internationalize your campus, you will have much to learn, and you will have a great deal of responsibility. If you are on a campus where staff members and experience in internationalizing the campus are scarce, you will have a particularly steep learning curve. The road map presented in this chapter provides you with the milestones you can use to gauge your progress as you travel the road to internationalize your campus.

References

Hoffa, W., and Pearson, J. *NAFSA's Guide to Education Abroad for Advisers and Administrators.* (2nd ed.) Washington, D.C.: NAFSA: Association of International Educators, 1997.

Rawson, G. *Immigration Classifications and Legal Employment of Foreign Nationals in the States.* Washington, D.C.: NAFSA: Association of International Educators, 2001.

BETH H. CARMICAL *is director of the Multi-Cultural Center and International Student Life at the University of North Carolina at Pembroke and serves as the FOCUS editor for the North Carolina Association of International Educators.*

INDEX

Back Issue/Subscription Order Form

Copy or detach and send to:

Jossey-Bass, A Wiley Company, 989 Market Street, San Francisco CA 94103-1741

Call or fax toll free: Phone 888-378-2537 6AM-5PM PST; Fax 888-481-2665

Back issues: Please send me the following issues at $27 each

(Important: please include series initials and issue number, such as HE114)

1. HE _____

_____

_____

$ _____ Total for single issues

$ _____ SHIPPING CHARGES: SURFACE

	Domestic	Canadian
First Item	$5.00	$6.50
Each Add'l Item	$3.00	$3.00

For next-day and second-day delivery rates, call the number listed above.

Subscriptions: Please ❑ start ❑ renew my subscription to *New Directions for Higher Education* for the year 2_____ at the following rate:

U.S.	❑ Individual $60	❑ Institutional $131
Canada	❑ Individual $60	❑ Institutional $171
All Others	❑ Individual $84	❑ Institutional $205

$ _____ Total single issues and subscriptions (Add appropriate sales tax for your state for single issue orders. No sales tax for U.S. subscriptions. Canadian residents, add GST for subscriptions and single issues.)

Federal Tax ID 135593032   GST 89102 8052

❑ Payment enclosed (U.S. check or money order only)

❑ VISA, MC, AmEx, Discover Card # _____ Exp. date_____

Signature _____ Day phone _____

❑ Bill me (U.S. institutional orders only. Purchase order required)

Purchase order #_____

Name _____

Address _____

_____

Phone_____ E-mail _____

For more information about Jossey-Bass, visit our Web site at: www.josseybass.com

PROMOTION CODE = ND3

HE95   **An Administrator's Guide for Responding to Campus Crime: From Prevention to Liability**
Richard Fossey, Michael Clay Smith
Provides advice on crime prevention programs, campus police training, rape prevention, fraud in federal grant programs, and the problems associated with admitting students with criminal backgrounds.
ISBN: 0-7879-9873-7